HOW TO OPEN AND RUN A MONEY-MAKING

TRAVEL AGENCY

Pamela Fremont

A Wiley Press Book
John Wiley & Sons, Inc.

New York • Chichester • Brisbane • Toronto • Singapore

Publisher: Judy V. Wilson
Editor: Alicia Conklin
Managing Editor: Maria Colligan
Composition and make up: Cobb-Dunlop Publisher
Services, Inc.

Library of Congress Cataloging in Publication Data:

Fremont, Pamela
   How to open and run a money-making
   travel agency.

   Bibliography: p. 197
   Includes index.
   1. Travel agents—Vocation guidance. I. Title.
G154.F73   1983   910.4'068   83-3517
ISBN 0-471-89335-8

Printed in the United States of America

10 9 8 7 6

HOW TO OPEN AND RUN A MONEY-MAKING

TRAVEL AGENCY

To the Fremont family
not forgetting
Alphonse and Jason.

Contents

Acknowledgment

My thanks to Joanne Caputo for typing the early stages of the book, and to Marissa Panigrosso for helping to put the final version on paper. My special thanks to my daughter Madeleine for her strong support and help throughout.

Foreword

Is there a thrill in the world that matches stepping off a plane in a foreign capital knowing that you will be wined and dined by VIPs there, that you will be shown everything you ask to see, that you will be an honored guest staying in the finest hotel? For some people there is one joy that might be even greater—making lots of money.

Well, now you can do both at the same time.

Does this sound impossible?

What image comes to your mind at the mention of the words *travel agent*? A harassed, tired, overworked, and underpaid individual sitting behind a desk piled high with files and brochures in a tiny, cramped office? It's too true. Too many agents fit this depressing description.

But it does not have to be. That is not the way to enjoy this exciting job and all its unbelievable benefits. That is not the way to get your share of the large sums of money generated by the giant travel industry.

I am well qualified to discuss this industry and help you become a qualified travel agent. I have been in the travel business for over seventeen years, first as a sales agent, then as office manager of travel agencies. I have obtained official agency appointment for a new travel agency and I have trained many classes of travel agents. I know the travel agency business from every point of view, and after seventeen years I still find it the most exciting job in the world.

In this book I will discuss the travel industry in today's world of economic problems. I will show you in actual figures the money earned in the last five years by the travel agencies in the United States. I will discuss the deregulation of the airlines and the proposed deregulation of travel agencies. You will learn how to make money as an agent with or without deregulation.

We will also talk about *you*. Together we will decide if you would be happy and would prosper as a travel agent.

I will then show you, easily, step by step, how to open your own travel agency, representing the airlines, shipping lines, hotels, Amtrak, and car rentals. This usually difficult-to-obtain information is clearly laid out for you. You will learn how to set up your agency in the most efficient way to run your business smoothly and profitably. You will learn how to build your business far beyond the dreams of most agents.

Even if you decide that agency ownership is not your ambition, you will learn about the various parts of the giant travel and tourist industry, how they mesh together—and where you can fit in, if you so decide, and become a part of it all.

All costs quoted in this book are subject to change—membership fees, prices, and subscriptions. Addresses and telephone numbers are provided so that you can check at the time you wish to apply the information.

1

The Anatomy
of a Travel Agency

What do you think of when you hear the words "travel industry"? For most of us, it's the people who take our reservations—the travel agent or airline ticket agent. Or maybe we think of the smartly uniformed flight crews who smile out at us from all the commercials. But the travel industry encompasses more than travel agents or even airline personnel. When you reserve a rental car or a hotel room, you are dealing with members of the travel industry. Cruise ships and transatlantic crossings comprise still another segment. Government tourist offices—even passport and visa offices—can also be said to be part of the vast travel industry.

And behind all these big labels—airlines, ships, hotels, and so on—lies an entire network of support services and regulatory bodies. Without the contribution of these groups, travel can slow down or even come to a standstill. Examples of how the lack of support services can hinder travel are the air traffic controllers' strike in 1981, which seriously slowed down airline schedules, and the walkout of cleaning staff unions in San Francisco hotels, which dealt a crushing blow to the travel market and economy of northern California in the summer of 1980.

Thus, the travel industry is a large network of people interacting at various levels to keep the flow of passengers moving safely and happily in a minimum amount of time. So where does the travel agency belong in the overall scheme of the travel world?

A travel agency serves the needs of airlines, hotels, tour operators, ships, and other forms of transportation by making its services available to vacationers and businesspeople who want to travel. A travel agency can free both a corporation president and a mother with four children from having to call for reservations for hotels, planes, or cars. By contacting their agent, travelers can have all the details and arrangements of travel taken care of—for no extra charge!

The absence of a service charge for the client is what makes a travel agency so unique. A travel agency actually serves two clients: the customer going on a trip and the airline or hotel used by the customer. But this double service is paid for by the suppliers of travel services, not by the customer.

The travel services compensate an agency for giving them business by paying a commission for each booking. Every segment has standard rates by which the agency is paid: for example, airlines and hotels pay 8 to 10 percent. The agency is compensated for the bookings, and the recipient of the booking makes money because the agency selected its services over those of everyone else. An agency's income comes from these commissions.

This system gives an agent a feeling of worth, and even to a certain extent, power. If an airline, for example, has denied confirmation of your reservation or been extremely rude to your passengers, you can give future bookings to competing airlines. Needless to say, airlines are not unaware of this possibility, and they have taken steps to enhance their image and solve problems before there are any negative ramifications.

For instance, airlines assign representatives to various geographical territories. These people visit all the travel agencies in that territory and try to sort out any difficulties. This system provides a personal contact in the airline to whom agents can turn when necessary.

One important aspect of the travel industry is often overlooked by the casual observer: regulation. Airlines, shipping lines, and travel agencies have been carefully watched over by various government agencies for many years. These regulatory agencies are there to protect the public from swindlers; they also encourage the travel industry to achieve uniformity in their operations in order to protect them from nuisance lawsuits. If there is one thing a travel agency must do, it is to conform to the rules set out by the government agencies responsible for this area of travel. Those rules provide the only assurance your customers have that you are honest and that the tickets you issue are valid and will be honored.

To appreciate the role of the agent and the agency in the travel industry as a whole, we need to look more closely at the work a travel agency actually does. Let's begin with a look at a typical travel agent's day.

A DAY IN THE LIFE OF A TRAVEL AGENT

No two days in a travel agency are completely identical, but some things happen almost every day.

9:00 A.M.

Coffee's brewing. Office is quiet, since we don't open for half an hour yet. Came in early to check files before the rush begins. Have been going through the mail. The trade paper, *The Travel Agent*, is in; will leave it on my desk to look at as soon as I can. Mail brings hotel confirmations, lots of brochures, a postcard from a client in Bangkok. I attach the confirmations to the worksheets in the files; add the brochures to the pile for the part-time help to imprint with the agency's stamp and put in the information file.

Good—the new *Official Airline Guide* is in. We'll be up-to-date with the changes in flight times. New guides go on the desks; the old ones go to outside salespersons to take home. Now for a look at the file of today's "tickets to be picked up." Quite a pile. I'd better write the ones that have not been done yet. It'll be a busy day.

11:00 A.M.

New client just breezed in. He's working on a construction job and has a few days off, starting tomorrow. He wants some gambling. No trouble getting him on a flight to Las Vegas tomorrow morning. He seems to go to Vegas regularly and knows where he wants to stay. Called hotel representative and got confirmation of a room. Wrote his ticket and hotel voucher. So he's all set. Cash sale.

Read in *The Travel Agent* that fares for New York to San Francisco will go up the day after tomorrow. Checked the files of a family we have booked to go there next month. They're all paid up, so immediately wrote their tickets to protect them from the fare increase.

Called Mrs. A. to tell her. She'll be in around lunchtime to pick up the tickets.

Young couple came in to tell me how much they enjoyed the snorkeling in St. Thomas. Nice of them to tell me. I knew they would have a great time since that's a wonderful spot for snorkeling.

12:15 P.M.

Secretary from legal office next door just picked up cruise ticket. I've never seen her so excited. She should be too. We got her a really nice cabin at a great rate.

Terrific! The vacation club at the chemical company has decided to go on a ten-day trip to the Canadian Rockies. I'm glad I suggested it. Their spokesperson sounded really enthusiastic. Twenty people is quite a big group. I think I'll send one of the staff out with them as tour escort. I'll bring it up at the next staff meeting.

2:00 P.M.

Mrs. A. came in. She had just bought herself a suit for San Francisco. Trip really means a lot to her. Keeps telling us how much she'll miss her sons now that they are finishing school and going off to college. Well, the family will have a good time together in California first.

Another student from the university called in for flights. Have had about seven of them this morning. They must have just received their examination schedules. As soon as the exams are over they head home. This one asked me if it was all right for her parents in the Midwest to send a check for her ticket. Fine, as long as the check gets here before she wants to pick up her ticket.

Haven't had lunch yet. Time for a sandwich, coffee, and a look at the newspaper. The dollar is really up this week, especially against the French franc. I've got clients in Paris now. That will help their shopping and the restaurant tabs. I'll tear out the currency exchange chart and put it on the notice board. That makes it easier to convert when hotel rates are quoted in foreign currency. There's trouble in central and east Africa. Better select safari areas carefully and keep our clients out of trouble.

4:00 P.M.

Air France's representative for this area has just been in. Just back from Tahiti. Looked fabulous. I reviewed with him a refund I have claimed for a client who lost his airline ticket in Paris and had to purchase a one-way ticket home. Air France is having a cocktail reception at the Hilton next Thursday to introduce its new package tours. Put it on the calendar and posted it on the notice board so that the staff will be sure to see it.

One of our business accounts, a printing company, has just called. The manager has to be on the first flight to Phoenix tomorrow morning. His reservation requests always come in at the last moment, but I know exactly what he wants: first class on the flight, Oldsmobile Cutlass at the airport, and downtown hotel. I'll get everything in order and drop off his ticket on my way home.

5:30 P.M.

No real problems left unsolved. There are still two flights in Texas not yet confirmed on Dr. J's itinerary. I'll talk to Delta tomorrow and see if they have cleared by then.

The cash tallies. The bank deposit is ready. I'll take that with me too; no use leaving money in the office overnight.

Two weeks from today I'll be in Hong Kong. I can hardly wait! It's six years since I was there. Last time I stayed at the Excelsior; this time it will be the Peninsula Hotel. They're both beautiful. And all that wonderful food!

Before I lock up let me look at tomorrow's calendar. Oh, yes! Pacific Tours breakfast seminar at the Marriott. I want brochures on the Australian and New Zealand tours and the new rate sheet for the South Sea Islands.

That's it for today.

As you can see, travel agents deal with all types of people with differing needs. But there are three main kinds. There are those who know exactly what they want and merely need your services to take care of the particulars. Then there are the clients who rely totally on the agent's advice. And there is a third type, those who really want more than advice. They are looking for a destination, and, unspoken, they want reassurance that taking a trip is what they should do, as well as that this is the place they should go. You, as the agent, can't solve their personal problems or their longings, but you can try to assess what they need and at least provide the best possible setting for their dreams.

A GALLERY OF CLIENTS

The typical day we just outlined involved several typical clients and their needs. Let's take a closer look at them, to see how you as the agent can help them.

The Las Vegas Client

He knows exactly where he wants to go, where to stay, and what he's going to do there. He's done it all before. His is the easiest type of booking. Just make his reservation and give him his documents. The only extra service you could add is to look at the Las Vegas entertainment section in the trade magazine and tell him who is performing in the show at his hotel.

The St. Thomas Couple

Their vacation is over and was obviously successful. It sounds from today's visit as if they also knew the type of vacation activity they wanted—snorkeling. They needed advice on where to find this sport, as well as on other aspects of their holiday. As their agent you would have looked for a hotel that draws a young clientele, has a good beach, and above all, has good snorkeling facilities in a prime area.

The Secretary

She's going off on her precious two-weeks-a-year vacation and she wants to make the most of every minute. She hopes to meet some young companions to have fun with on the cruise. You help her by choosing a ship that is a favorite with the young crowd and by advising her to sit at a large table in the dining room so that she can get a head start at meeting people. She made this reservation months in advance, and she has been thinking of it daily since you told her her cabin was confirmed. She asked your advice on clothes to bring, and you described shipboard life: the casual daytime—swimming and deck sports or sightseeing on shore; the dress-up, gala evenings of dining, dancing, and entertainment. She's already on board in her imagination. It's always rewarding to help enthusiastic travelers.

The Vacation Club

These people are somewhat like the secretary, but multiplied by twenty. It's that multiplication that brings in the complications. They work in the same company, but it is a large one and they may not know each other well. Spouses will also be along. This group will need leadership.

As their agent you have attended their last planning meeting and given them suggestions. You gave two detailed plans with costs—the Canadian trip and an alternative. Now that the group has decided to go to Canada, you will choose a member of your staff as tour guide and take that person with you to the group's next meeting. It is during the tour that the group will emerge as individuals. (Later in the book we will go into the details of escorting a group.)

The Family Going to San Francisco

Obviously Mrs. A. has high expectations of this trip. She's family-oriented and values the time she can spend with her relatives. She has a touch of wistfulness and belongs in our category of people for whom more than the actual trip is involved. As her agent you've chosen well. San Francisco is a perfect background for a vacation that will be entered into family memories.

You've told her to take the bay cruise, walk in Muir Woods, wander around Fisherman's Wharf, browse in the little shops in Ghiradelli Square. I hope you also told her to take a camera so that in later years Mrs. A. can point to her photographs and say, "Here I am in San Francisco with the flowers the boys bought me from the flower vendor on the street corner." This family means more to you than four transcontinental airline tickets.

The Students

They're studying for exams, so they don't have time to come to the agency. The reservation requests come over the phone. Don't be too surprised if several of them call back to cancel because they have found a ride home. Just have the tickets ready when it's time for them to go. You'll meet them again next semester. And maybe when they have graduated they just might settle in your community.

The Business Manager

His reservations are taken care of by phone by his secretary. You've probably met him once, briefly. But you know exactly what you need to know. You have his likes and dislikes on file, where he likes to sit on the plane, and his special food preferences. This is clear-cut business. It is one of your commercial accounts, and you live up to every promise of service you made. *Of course* you'll drop off that ticket at his office.

Just a typical day—but the clients represent all three of the groups previously mentioned. Is anyone left from our day's visitors? Yes, the Air France representative.

We go into the duties of airline representatives and how they can be helpful to you later in the book. The representatives are in and out of your office quickly, and they are welcome visitors. The agent feels relaxed when talking to representatives, for they are people in the same industry. They visit agents all day and know both the important news and the good gossip. No wonder they're welcome!

Now we have discussed all the people we met during the day. But there's one important item still to be mentioned—the daily newspaper.

The news around the world affects your job as an agent and your clients. You don't have to be a political expert, but you must be aware of what is going on and where. Know where that military takeover occurred, where martial law was just declared, where there has been an outbreak of typhoid fever. Note the special festivals—Olympics, world fairs, art festivals, sports events. Know enough not to send your clients into trouble. Just read the newspaper daily. The major trouble spots appear in the front two pages. Never skip the international section. You don't need to know all the details, but you must be aware of the general picture and how events are likely to affect your travelers. As a travel agent, the whole world is your business.

THE AGENT'S RESPONSIBILITIES

Travel differs from other businesses in that the agent has nothing tangible to sell—only a promise of service. When your clients walk out of your agency with their airline tickets they receive only a written promise that the airline will carry them from point A to point B. If they were to arrive at the airport and be refused seats on the plane in exchange for their tickets, they would be holding worthless pieces of paper. But there is a very big difference between an authorized airline ticket and a discarded candy wrapper. The difference is the word *authorized*. Clients cannot sit at their desks at home and write airline tickets for themselves. Only the airlines themselves and authorized agents, who have met required standards of knowledge and maintain honorable business practices, can write tickets for airline travel, and that fact guarantees that those tickets will be honored for passage on the flights specified.

Obviously there must be a person or body overseeing the practice of ticket distribution to ensure that unauthorized tickets (forgeries) are not being circulated and that the agents authorized to sell tickets are doing so in accordance with regulations. Such bodies do exist, and because of their importance to the travel industry and agencies in particular, the next chapter will be devoted to a detailed look at them.

Travel is a strictly controlled industry, as it should be. As an agent you are in a position of trust. Clients have trusted you by paying for transportation before they have received it. Airlines trust you by allowing you to receive money for services they will perform. It is obvious that there must be a regular schedule whereby the airlines receive payment from the agents. In fact these payments are made weekly in the form of the agency sales report, of which you will hear more later. You will work within regulations that ensure that you perform ethically for both your clients and the airlines, shipping lines, or other providers of services.

As an agent your basic responsibilities are these:

- You request space from the carrier only when requested by a client to do so.

- You charge the client the fare established by the carrier, as quoted to you at time of making the reservation or as set forth in the tariff manual.
- You at all times use the lowest applicable fare for the service requested by the passenger.
- You do not make duplicate reservations for the same journey.
- You immediately cancel with the carrier any reservation the passenger cancels with you.
- You pay the carrier weekly, by means of the agency's sales report, for the transportation and related services provided by the carriers.

These responsibilities do not seem too onerous. When you consider them, they are simply reasonable business standards.

There is another very important point. As an agent, you must retain your objectivity and impartiality in making choices for your clients. When asked for a flight reservation, choose the airline that gives the service most convenient for the passenger. The agent receives the same commission regardless of which carrier he or she selects. This objectivity belongs only to the agent and is an extremely good reason for clients to use agency services instead of calling each airline in turn, using up a great deal of their own time. You might well come to prefer dealing with one particular airline where possible, but never do so to the extent of compromising your most valuable asset—your objectivity. This impartiality, together with your educated judgment, is what sets you apart as a travel expert. It applies not only to airlines but to shipping lines, hotels, car rental companies, and in fact, every service that you represent.

THE AGENT'S ADVANTAGES

Now to a very pleasant part of your job as an agent—the benefits you derive.

Yes, you really do have the entire world available to you for your own travel. You would have to be a millionaire to equal an agent's travel privileges. It is an enormous advantage and a great joy.

The travel benefits are given for a reason. It is a great help to be familiar with what you are selling. It is impossible to recommend a hotel if you know neither the hotel nor the area in which it is located. To keep up to date, travel agents frequently take what are called familiarization trips.

Familiarization trips are exactly what the name implies. They are frequently sponsored jointly by an airline and a hotel chain and sometimes a national tourist office for the purpose of acquainting the agent with the carrier's flight service to the area, the area itself, and the hotel and other services located there. On these trips your time is usually fully occupied in visiting hotels and going on sightseeing tours. The days are full and tiring but enormously enjoyable. As you become used to these trips, you become more adept at gathering the information that is likely to be most useful for your particular clientele. These times spent getting acquainted with a foreign country are working days for the agent. They are the same as the days your clients pay to enjoy, except that the agent moves faster, sees more, and definitely checks out more hotels. I wouldn't call these trips pure joy rides; but I'll settle for "exceptionally enjoyable work." An added plus: any of your own money that you spend on these trips (other than personal shopping) is deductible from your income tax.

Familiarization trips are not, however, the only enviable part of an agent's job. A very active social life also comes with the job, often under the heading of "seminars." These can take the form of breakfast, lunch, cocktails, or dinner. The usual procedure is to have the social activity first, followed by time for the agents to talk and then a film presentation or a talk related to the host's product.

It's a full, busy life, both inside and outside of the office. Can *you* think of any other job where every corner of the world is on the "must visit" list?

2

Should *You* Open a Travel Agency?

Well, does a travel agent's life appeal to you so far?

You love to travel; you might even have thought of opening a travel agency many times but didn't because you were not sure what was involved, whether you could handle the work, or whether you could make a living doing it. So let's take a look at the skills and resources you need to be a travel agent.

JOB SKILLS FOR A TRAVEL AGENT

In the last chapter we talked of agents' dealings with, and relationship to, their clients. Clients are your fundamental responsibility: they are your work; they are your income. The work sheets in your file cabinets are simply lists of your clients' needs, with notations of which have been taken care of and which have not. Thus, the prime requirement of the travel agent is the ability to understand people and communicate easily with them. You must inspire them with total confidence in your ability to take care of them. You must have the self-confidence to tell them bad news. For example, when the hotel they have their heart set on is totally sold out, you must be able to say so and proceed from there to an acceptable alternative. They must always feel that your knowledge will ensure the success of their trip.

Have you ever held a job in which you deal directly with the public? It is the same public you will deal with whether you are a doctor, librarian, salesperson, or travel agent. Travel agents are, of course, the most fortunate: their public is going on vacation and is in a happy mood when dealing with you. But the travel agent should have certain traits and attitudes that encourage successful relationships with the public, whatever mood they are in. There are ways to judge whether you have such skills.

- You have had such a job already.
- You enjoyed certain courses in school (social studies, for example).
- You gravitate to people-oriented work, no matter what official position you hold.

Here are some other attributes that would be useful to have if you want to pursue life as a travel agent:

- A business which already has a list of clientele.
- Business sense or know-how acquired from past jobs.

- Imagination and ability to generate business.
- Membership in religious or social groups—a source of clients.
- Patience for detailed work.
- Ability to work under stress.
- Ability to work within industry regulations.
- Good educational background with special interest in geography and world events.

The absence of some of these attributes, however, should not keep you from entering the field. Enthusiasm and intuition more than equal the characteristics just listed. Success can be achieved by your own capabilities in running your agency. But don't decide to open an agency solely on one strength in your background. Weigh several factors.

If at present you own a law practice, an insurance agency, or a real estate agency, you have a ready-made clientele for your travel agency. You will require only enough space and enough hands to accommodate the new business, and the additional income will be yours. In fact, your travel agency will find new clients who can be added to your list of customers in your present business. One business fuels the other.

Are you getting close to your retirement? Are you wondering what you will do with the unoccupied time ahead of you? Does freedom to travel all over the world appeal to you? Would you like to learn a new business? Your previous years of business or professional experience will be a valuable background for your travel career. I cannot think of any business more exciting or rewarding for a couple in retirement than the travel industry. The great advantage is that once your agency is established, you can make your own hours—full time, part time, or even just a few hours a week. It's all up to you. The only "complaint" comes from grown-up children who claim that their parents are now too busy and happy to babysit.

START-UP COSTS

If you open an agency you will find, that, as with any business, there are start-up costs. These costs vary according to your region and community, size of the agency, and to some extent, your own ambition. Outside of the long but flexible list of necessities required for any business, there are rigid requirements for travel agencies that must be met first.

When you first open your agency you will not be able to collect commissions from airlines and shipping reservations until you have been officially appointed by regulating conferences. You will then receive retroactive commissions for the sales you made in the waiting period. Therefore, you must be able to survive during this period, usually thirty to ninety days for airline sales. You can, however, collect hotel and car rental commissions from the beginning.

If you yourself do not qualify by having two years' experience selling air and shipping travel and writing tickets, you must hire someone who does. Salaries will vary according to geographical areas. Talk to employment agencies, and if possible, other travel agents nearby to establish the appropriate salaries for an office manager in your area.

Fees and Bonds

An Air Traffic Conference (ATC) bond in the amount of $10,000 is a performance or guaranty type of bond and may be placed with any surety or bonding company included in the list issued by the U.S. Treasury Department. (Regulating bodies will be discussed in Chapter 5.) A bond application form can be obtained from ATC. You can discuss with the bonding company what collateral it will require: cash, property, or other assets. Your bank manager can be helpful too, particularly if the bank has handled your account for a number of years.

Fees for applications to conferences and annual agency fees after appointment are as follows:

Air Traffic Conference

- Application fee $200
- Annual agency fee   200

International Air Traffic Association

- Application fee $ 50
- Entrance fee   200
- Annual agency fee   35

International Passenger Ship Association

- Application fee $ 25
- Annual agency fee   40

Cruise Conference

- Application fee (as listed at time of application)
- Annual agency fee $ 42.50

Office facilities

Telephones

The telephone is the lifeline of your agency. It is the source of much of your incoming business, and it is also your means of securing reservations for your clients.

Representatives of any telephone system will come to your office and discuss with you a system that suits both your business and your budget. If you are new to the agency field and are keeping costs as low as possible in starting up your office, a safe move would be to start with a minimum of three telephones, three consecutive numbers, and a hold button. As time goes on you will have a better idea of what type of phone system you will need. You will also have attained the volume of business to warrant a more elaborate phone system as well as the capital to invest in it.

Safe

This is actually a requirement of the Air Traffic Conference. You will need a burglar-proof steel safe bolted to the floor (of which more will be said in the next chapter).

Safety Deposit Box

Another requirement of ATC is the use of a bank safety deposit box to store your ticket supply. Choose the nearest bank to your agency.

File Cabinets

You will need at least four file cabinets. One will be in your front office and should blend with your decor. This is where you will keep your work files. The remaining three files will be in your back office and used for filing brochures in geographical order. You will add to the number of file cabinets you use when you require storage files.

Desks

Start with at least three. A standard secretary-type desk with a right-angle table for a typewriter is the most convenient. You need chairs, too, one for each desk and a few for clients.

Typewriters

You'll want one for each desk if you can afford them. If not, get one good typewriter to start with and add others when you can.

Stationery

You'll need some items with your agency letterhead:

- Writing paper and envelopes.
- Invoices.
- Receipt books.
- Speed memos.

And some without your letterhead:

- Work sheets—order a thousand.
- Message pads.
- Industry manuals and essential books (these are listed in Chapter 5 along with their costs).

How much money will you need to open an agency? Obviously there can be no one answer for different areas and different intentions. Also, the figure required will be much higher if an office manager has to be hired because you cannot fill this position yourself. In estimating the capital you will require, you should base your costs on a full year's operating expenses. True, the agency will provide income, but any service business takes time to establish—a reputation cannot be built overnight.

Assuming rent of $1,000 per month, purchase of furniture and equipment just listed, insurance, utilities, telephone bills, application costs to conferences and one year's dues, and one year's subscription to manuals and periodicals, and assuming your ability to obtain the $10,000 bond, I would estimate a figure of $30,000, plus salaries, if any. Can it be done for less? Smaller premises might be rented for $600 per month (there are areas where costs will be considerably lower). There can be a saving in buying used furniture and equipment. Call around and price the items in your area, according to your own taste and financial ability. Don't be over-whelmed because you can't afford a lot to start with. Stick to the minimums. Luxury and generosity can be a plant and an open dish of candy. Your enthusiasm and ability to work remain the greatest essentials.

The availability of financing depends more on the national economy than the type of business you plan to undertake. Banks look favorably on two factors when they consider financing—the applicants' knowledge of and experience in the business and their success and reliability in previous business undertakings. There are many ways to approach the financial aspects. If you have cash in hand and can swing the entire operation—congratulations! If not, your local bank should be your first stop. If it helps finance you, you will give it your business accounts in return.

A NOTE ON TRAVEL AND TODAY'S ECONOMY

You are aware of current problems of inflation, recession, and unemployment, and you probably think that as a consequence, the travel business is suffering, too.

However, according to *Travel Weekly*, June 23, 1980, in the six months from January to June 1979, travel agents sold $7 billion in airline bookings. In the first six months of 1980, ATC of America reported travel agency sales at $9.4 billion, a 33 percent *increase* in one year. Commissions for 1980 sales amounted to $745 million, 34 percent greater than the previous year. From January through June of 1976, before the present recession started, agents' commissions totaled $329 million, less than half the figure earned in air commissions by agents in 1980.

Have your profits in your present business more than doubled in the last four years?

While we're dealing in facts and figures let's look at just how rapidly the air traffic market has grown.

- In 1948, 183,000 Americans crossed the Atlantic.
- In 1952, this figure doubled.
- In 1960, it redoubled.
- In 1968, it increased tenfold.
- In 1979, the total was over four million, more than twenty-two times the 1948 total.

Make no mistake: air travel is here to stay and will continue to grow.

The Louis Harris report commissioned by *Travel Weekly* released figures for 1981 events and vacations which show the travel agency market to be among the top nine growth industries in the country. From 1970 to 1981 it has grown 520 percent, producing total sales of $31 billion in 1981—a year when many industries suffered heavy losses.

WHY DO PEOPLE TRAVEL?

People today are going to travel, either for business or for pleasure. Pleasure can mean a vacation away from the pressures of business and to enjoy a new area or it can mean a visit to friends or relatives who live in another corner of the world.

As recently as seventy-five years ago, most people grew up, married, and settled down in the area where they were born. Their businesses, their relatives, and their friends were all close around them. Annual holidays were spent in the same place each summer—at the shore or in the mountains—usually the vacation spot nearest to home and reachable by bus or train. Travel, as such, was for the wealthy only. Ships carried only rich adventurers and, many decks below, immigrants on one long journey to another part of the world, seeking a life not available in their own land.

Think, in contrast, of today's travelers. Secretaries and students are going to Bermuda. Your neighbors are going to Mexico. Young people who have just graduated from high school are spending six weeks in Europe. Travel is available to everyone today, and the taste for travel, once acquired, does not disappear. Vacation travel has become a habit, and business travel a necessity. This is why travel is a huge, ever-growing business and will continue to be a source of healthy profits.

In the September 8, 1980, issue of *U.S. News and World Report*, a barometer of American business, an article entitled "Americans Play Even with Economy in Spin" says, "Consumers who are pinching pennies on essential items are shelling out hard earned cash for such amusement as sporting events and vacations." It is estimated that $218 billion will be spent on recreation this year, nearly four times the amount spent fifteen years ago. Right now, one dollar out of every eight earned in this country goes for leisure activities—a larger share than for housing, construction, and national defense. "That spending is important to a healthy economy," says

Douglas Frechtling, director of United States Travel Data Center. "When people cut back, the vacation is usually the last item to go. People count on it and plan on it. It's the time to relax and not worry about spending." In good times or bad travelers are there and ready to go.

3

The Powers That Be

REGULATORY AGENCIES

To understand the world of a travel agent, you need to be introduced to the various regulatory agencies that govern the travel industry. Each area of transportation is governed by its own conference rulings.

Since the greatest part of an agent's work depends on air travel, let's start with that part of the industry.

Air travel is strictly regulated, as it must be, since the lives of millions of passengers are at stake. Here are the controlling bodies (federal agencies are generally referred to by their initials not only by the industry but also by newspapers and trade publications.):

Federal Aviation Association (FAA)

This is the federal agency most responsible for civil aviation. It was established in 1958, and in 1967 became a part of the Department of Transportation. Its purposes are to regulate air commerce and oversee aviation safety and to promote civil aviation and a national system of airports. It establishes efficient use of navigable airspace. Also it develops and operates a common system of air traffic control and air navigation for both civil and military aircraft.

You have heard many times of federal investigations into airplane crashes. It is the FAA that reconstructs events to find the cause. If more than one aircraft was involved, the FAA establishes if there was a violation of the system of travel flow. (Planes must be separated by 3 miles, or 4.8 kilometers, in distance and a thousand feet, 305 meters, in altitude from other aircraft.)

Other roles of the FAA include setting standards for qualifications of airline pilots, conducting periodic inspection of pilots' proficiency, and accepting standards of airworthiness for all civil aircraft.

The FAA must approve the plans, design, engineering, and performance of all new types of planes. It does this task with great care. Aircraft manufacturers have known years of frustration while awaiting FAA approval of a new plane, as in the case of the 767.

Civil Aeronautics Board (CAB)

This is an independent regulatory agency, originally established under the Civil Aeronautics Act of 1938 and continued by the FAA.

This agency regulates the civil air transport industry within the United States and between the United States and foreign countries. Its role is mainly to oversee the carriers. It approves or disapproves proposed mergers, acquisition of control, or agreements between air carriers. The Airline Deregulation Act of 1978 greatly reduced the powers of the CAB. It will in fact cease to exist at the end of 1984, when its functions will be transferred to other agencies. Before 1978 two of its important functions were to grant licenses to carriers to provide air transportation on required routes and to approve rates and fares. In fact the CAB's authority over fares ended on December 31, 1982.

The CAB chooses U.S. carriers to serve between the United States and foreign countries where U.S. carrier entry is limited. The CAB is concerned with both carriers and travel agents to ensure that they do not engage in unfair and deceptive methods in the sale of air transportation services.

Air Transportation Association of America (ATA)

The members of this association are domestic trunk airlines, local service airlines, and air cargo airlines transporting persons, goods, and mail by aircraft between fixed points on a regular schedule. This agency, founded in 1936, is mainly administrative. It maintains a library of transportation texts and legal histories of civil aviation. It is important to travel agencies in that it oversees their administration. The department of ATA that directly concerns agents is the ATC.

Air Traffic Conference (ATC)

Its members include U.S. flag, scheduled, certified air carriers, including trunk airlines, local service carriers, and intra-Hawaii and intra-Alaska airlines. ATC was established in 1938. Its main purpose is to improve service to the air traveler, and it is in this capacity that it has become the agency dealt with most frequently by travel agents. It is to ATC that one applies for a license to become an authorized travel agent in the domestic market. It also publishes the *Travel Agents Handbook.*

International Air Traffic Association (IATA)

This agency was founded in 1945. Its members are scheduled international airline operators, and its associate members are the scheduled airlines in domestic service. It promotes safe, regular, and economical international air service; studies the problems of air commerce; and provides means of collaboration among air transport enterprises. This agency serves the same functions internationally as ATA does domestically. It is to the IATA that an agent applies for authorization to sell international airline tickets.

These are the conferences and associations travel agents are most concerned with. Other conferences exist to supervise pilots, aircraft owners, air traffic controllers, cargo, and aircraft electronic and engineering firms. The members of these agencies mesh together to form the airline industry, the huge and complex network which moves passengers, baggage, and cargo around the world daily. Safe and smooth operation in this vast field requires both self-policing and the authority of the governing bodies just discussed.

There is a high level of cooperation among conference members. A passenger who misses a connection will be carried by the next airline servicing that route. A lost piece of baggage will be put on the next flight to its proper destination. This interchange is made possible by the rules governing member airlines, rules enforced by these conferences. Seldom in any other industry does one see more cooperation among competitors. It requires a high degree of self-discipline and intelligent cooperation from every member of the industry—airline president, pilot, flight attendant, travel agent—to move the passengers comfortably and swiftly from point A to point B, whether these points are separated by only a few miles or by oceans and continents. It all works for the benefit of the passenger.

International Passenger Ship Association (IPSA)

Its members include passenger shipping lines and cruise lines sailing from the East Coast of the United States and Canada. This agency oversees the standards of its members, regulates regulations between member shipping companies and agents, and supplies promotional material to agents.

Pacific Cruise Conference (PCC)

This conference includes members from eleven cruise companies sailing from Pacific coast ports. Formed in 1922, PCC supplies member agencies with promotional material as an aid to cruise sales and manages relations between members and agents.

National Railroad Passenger Corporation (NRPC)

Members are Amtrak and other railroads in the United States. This group oversees the interests of Amtrak and cooperating carriers in dealing with agents and tour operators.

These conferences are the organizations from whom you require accreditation in order to sell reservations for their members. They have power to review your agency if complaints are issued against you by other members or by members of the public. These reviews are similar to the examination of your original application for membership. In addition specific complaints will be investigated. Any action taken against you, if you are found to have conducted your business in violation of the rules of the conference, is open to appeal.

United States Travel and Tourism Association (USTTA)

This association was established by the National Tourism Policy Act in 1981. It advises the secretary of commerce on making and carrying out national tourism policy. Its objectives: to motivate travel agents and tour operators abroad to select U.S. destinations and provide information and services to prospective consumers, to coordinate U.S. and overseas tourism interests, and to stimulate demand for travel in the United States and abroad. It also helps international associations in the selection of U.S. locations for future meetings.

TRADE ASSOCIATIONS

The industry also has several associations that travel agents may join if they wish.

American Society of Travel Agents (ASTA)

Active membership is not confined to travel agents; tour operators can also belong. Established in 1931, ASTA describes itself as "the world's largest association of travel and tourism professionals." It represents the interests of its members to airlines, shipping lines, and the public; and it guards against fraud and misrepresentation by agencies. Most of the traveling public has heard of ASTA and has confidence in an agency displaying the ASTA logo.

Association of Retail Travel Agents (ARTA)

This trade group includes only retail travel agents, representing their interests with travel suppliers or airline carriers and shipping companies. When conference rules are being changed, ARTA protects the agent's point of view.

Local associations of travel agents also exist throughout the country. They usually consider local problems, industry problems in general, and conditions applying to local agents. Suppliers may offer members increased commissions for specific offerings. These associations also offer familiarization trips to their members, on which agents would most likely know their fellow passengers.

Travel marketing groups, a form of cooperative, were established to represent groups of wholesalers, suppliers, and agents. The agents are the outlet for the suppliers, generally at a higher commission rate than that paid to nonmembers. Increased commissions are not the only advantage of membership in these cooperatives. Because the suppliers who belong have been screened, the agents can believe in the quality of the services promised. The marketing group should not become so large as to defeat its purpose. Its existence is justified by its association of reputable suppliers and agents. Members are entirely free to do business with nonmembers as well as with the cooperative. One such travel marketing group is TravelSavers, which was established ten years ago and now has a membership of five hundred travel agencies and fifty suppliers.

Organizations are now being formed for users of specific types of automation. These give members an opportunity to compare results and problems and serve as a means of communication between agents and automation suppliers. One such organization is Travel Agent's Computer Society (TACOS) in Natwick, Massachusetts.

One further word concerning authorities: find out if your state requires licensing. This trend is growing and helps protect agents in general from the unfavorable public opinion that can be generated by a few unworthy agents.

4

Some Structural Preliminaries

There are two ways to set yourself up as a travel agent: you can buy an existing agency or open your own.

First, let's examine the pros and cons of buying an existing agency. (Chapter 5 is devoted entirely to how to open your own agency and the steps involved in becoming an appointed agent.)

Pro: BUYING AN EXISTING AGENCY

- No lag period without income.
- Faster return on investment.
- Clientele already established.
- Office already staffed.
- Office already physically equipped.
- Agency benefits not affected (but you will have to establish your own personal qualification).

Con:

- Will normally cost more than opening own agency.
- Financial notes to be paid off over a period of years if not outright cash purchase.
- Buying the faults along with the plusses.
- Employees selected by someone else. Will they all stay?

Before you decide to buy an agency you must find out the answers to the following important questions. These answers determine the selling price.

- What is the annual percentage of growth in sales volume and commissions?
- Are ATC and IATA appointments in good standing?
- Is the location desirable?
- What are the terms of the lease?
- Is the agency automated?
- How long has the agency been established?
- Does the agency have an all-round business or a particular specialty?
- How large is the staff? What are the salaries? How many will stay on under new ownership?

You should also consider and discuss with the present agency owner these points:

1. Do you want the present owner to stay on as manager until you qualify? If the owner is leaving, be sure

you have a contract that prevents him or her from opening another agency nearby within a period of several years. (If the owner were to do so, the clients would automatically move too, and you would have bought nothing).

2. If the physical furnishings are not to your liking, can they be excluded from the sale and their appraised value deducted from the purchase price?

3. Can you buy only a share in the agency or only a part of its business, rather than the whole operation? Would it be worthwhile to do so?

You should be guided in the purchase by your lawyer and perhaps accountant also. The present owner of the agency will be aware of ATC regulations for its sale, but it is advisable that you yourself be familiar with these requirements.

If you decide to buy an agency, various types of change of ownership are possible:

- Outright sale and change of ownership.
- Formation of a partnership or withdrawal of an existing partner.
- Incorporation of an agency that has not been previously incorporated.
- Sale of more than 10 percent of an agency's stock.

No less than forty five days from the intended date of change of ownership, you must send written notice to the Air Traffic Conference in Washington and the ATC bond insurer of the type of change that is to take place. Your notice to ATC should cover these points:

- Type of change intended.
- Date of proposed change.
- Name of present stockholder and names and addresses of all stockholders.
- Name and title of person who will meet the travel experience guidelines (two years) for the new owner, as well as background and qualifications.
- Whether either name or location of agency will be changed.
- Agency's ATC code number.

The ATC will immediately send you forms to facilitate the change of ownership.

A recent change in rules is beneficial to the new owner. Under present ruling, the ATC will take inventory of the current owner's ticket stock. When the change of ownership is approved (which must be within sixty days), the new owner will not, under the new ruling, be responsible for any obligation of the previous owner.

BUSINESS STRUCTURES

Whether you buy or open your own agency, you still must decide what structure your business will take: sole proprietorship, partnership, or corporation.

This is definitely a subject to discuss with your lawyer. Many factors must be weighed in choosing your form of business: your temperament, your finances, the amount of time you intend to devote to the job, your past experience in business. Income taxes differ according to the structure you choose, and your attorney should go over these with you. There are advantages and disadvantages in each situation.

Sole Proprietorship

The worries are yours alone—but so are the profits. If you have already worked in a travel agency, you should be able to assess whether you can handle sole ownership. If you are experienced in business, well organized, and confident of your ability to generate business, the outlook for you as a sole owner would be excellent. You will not have to cope with another person's opinions or the arguments resulting from different outlooks. Also, this is the easiest structure to set up. In a proprietorship you are totally and personally responsible for any liabilities incurred by the business. Your own possessions (home, car) could all be appropriated to cover liabilities. Your tax is paid on a personal basis on your agency income.

Partnership

A partnership, an agreement between two or more people to do business together, is the usual structure of travel agencies. These partnerships often take one of four forms.

First, there is partnership with someone who already has the two years' travel agency experience required. This saves the expense of hiring an experienced office manager. An ideal combination of talents is one partner with travel background and experience and the other with business and financial management knowhow.

Second, there is a partnership in which two or more people, each interested in travel, combine their energies and money to set up a business that provides an interesting job as well as unlimited travel for them and their spouses. The setup in this type of partnership is usually equal investment, equal division of work, and equal profits. However, when you are considering such a partnership, be sure the other people are as enthusiastic as you are. Are their business or job records good? Are you compatible? Do you respect each other's decisions?

The third form is a husband and wife partnership. I have already mentioned retired couples, but travel makes an excellent business partnership for couples of any age. It is important in this particular form of partnership that each person knows what to expect of the other. Are all duties to be done by both partners equally? Is one going to concentrate on selling while the other takes care of the bookkeeping and finances? Define roles at the outset, and go ahead with the partnership only if you're sure you can work together.

A fourth form of partnership is that between a person who does the actual work in the agency and a person who supplies the capital but does not work in the business. This form of partnership is often offered by a prospective financer to an agent who has established a reputation for knowledgeable work and has a loyal clientele. It is usual in this arrangement for decisions to be the prerogative of the working partner, unless they involve further investment of capital. The financial partner receives income from an agreed-on percentage of the profits.

The advantages or disadvantages of partnership are similar to those of proprietorship. Each partner is personally liable for debts of the business beyond its assets. The partnership itself does not pay taxes, although it is required to file a tax return. The partners pay tax on this income in their personal income tax return. It is advisable for a partnership agreement to be drawn up by a lawyer.

Corporation

This is the most formal and complex of the three possible ways to set up a business. Its main advantage is that once formed the corporation becomes an entity unto itself, and if losses are incurred beyond the total assets of the corporation, the person or persons owning the business are not personally liable. There are definite tax advantages and disadvantages, the most important of which is that the corporation pays income tax on its profits. The owners of the corporation must also declare their income from the business in their personal tax returns. This requirement is offset by tax advantages from the corporation's right to set up pension funds and health plans. More record keeping is required in a corporation than in the other forms, since there are taxes to be filed and stockholders to be answered to.

Corporations are governed by state law and therefore differ somewhat from state to state. If you decide to form a corporation, it is easier to do so from the beginning, for changing the form after the agency has been established involves filing for change of business status with the travel industry conferences as well as additional legal fees. A corporation can be formed regardless of whether the business is a sole proprietorship or a partnership.

Two facts disclosed in late 1982 from a survey of travel agencies conducted by the ATC will be of interest to those who are considering whether to open their own agency. (1) 75.3 percent of travel agencies are small businesses with annual sales of under $2 million. (2) Nearly half (45.8 percent) of all travel agencies in the United States are owned and controlled by women.

This is a much higher percentage of ownership and control by women than in other businesses, and although I do not know if any statistics exist on travel agency employees, I am sure that the percentage of women on agency staffs is extremely high. The field is especially attractive to women. I can think of innumerable agencies owned by women (individually or two women as partners) who have entered, or returned to, business after many years of raising families. One can become an agent without years spent in obtaining a degree, and the field certainly appears to be less resistant than other businesses to job seekers without a continuous record of employment.

The public accepts men or women as travel agents with equal ease. Whether banks, on being approached for start-up money, view women as equally good prospects is another matter—as it is for any other business venture. We have already discussed the criteria which would apply—experience and reliability.

SOME FINAL ADVICE

If at this point the idea of being an agency owner still appeals to you and you can afford the costs, I recommend one other step before you invest. Try to get a job in a travel agency. (Read Chapter 10, "Your Staff—How to Choose Them".) If this is not practical for you, look around and see if there are training programs open to the public in your area. You might find evening courses in your local community college. By gaining experience either practically or through education, you will have a sounder basis for making decisions.

Another, final point: is your interest in opening an agency based on business that will come from one large source? If so, beware. The industry conferences will not approve an agency in which more than 20 percent of the business is derived from one entity.

5

Opening Your Travel Agency

I cannot count how many times I have been asked, "How do I open a travel agency? Where do I begin? What do I have to do?" I have been asked these questions even by people who have been working in travel agencies for years. It seems to be a subject surrounded by mystery, one that is not discussed even in agencies themselves. Apparently one can be an agent for years and still have no idea how to go about establishing and building up an agency.

However, there is no mystery. Rather, you must follow a natural progression of events and requirements to create a working, accredited agency.

You can start with a bold and definite step: simply choose a location and prepare to open your business. It is necessary to get the business running and open to the public before applying to the certifying conferences for the appointment required for an agency to be placed on the official list.

As you read through the steps necessary to become an authorized agency, bear in mind the costs mentioned in Chapter 2. These steps reflect the implementation of the costs. Remember also that some of these steps can be done concurrently. They are set out here individually to insure that all the necessary requirements have been satisfied.

STEP 1: CHOOSE A LOCATION
AND OPEN YOUR AGENCY

There are some important things you should *not* do when you choose your location.

- Do *not* locate your agency in your own home, whether a house or an apartment. The agency must be located in a business premise, open and easily accessible to the public. The agency must remain open throughout regular business hours.

- Do *not* locate your agency in the same room as another business. If you already have an insurance or other type of business, you cannot have your travel agency in the same room. You must have one or more rooms used solely for the purpose of selling travel, and there must be an entrance from the street. If your office is located in a highrise commercial building, a door to the corridor can serve as access.

- Do *not* locate your office inside a hotel, unless you have direct access to the street. A hotel cannot have a financial interest in the business.

These are the ATC's official proscriptions. I have additional suggestions of my own:

- Select a busy commercial area so that you can get walk-in business. Do *not* choose an area where travel agencies already abound. You must be your own judge on this suggestion, since you are familiar with your own locality.
- Be sure there is adequate parking, unless you depend chiefly on foot traffic. If the other businesses that are already in the building take up an overly large share of the parking—for example, a doctor's office or beauty salon—before renting, get the agreed-on parking specifications for your office written into your lease.
- What are the zoning laws regarding signs? If the building is on a busy automobile route, a sign on the roof with the agency's name is effective advertising. Is that permitted?
- Are there middle- and upper-income homes within easy driving distance? These families could be your vacation business.
- Are there good-sized companies within a ten-mile radius that might provide business travel?
- Are you on the ground floor? This position is advantageous for walk-in business. If you are not on the ground floor, conferences require evidence of how you intend to generate business. A large street-level window is also a

draw when you display posters, ship models, and so on.

STEP 2: NAME YOUR AGENCY
AND PUT UP OUTDOOR SIGNS

If you are located in an office building where there are no exterior signs, list your agency in the office directory. Choose any name you want as long as the name is not the same as, or similar to, any other agency in the area. Avoid any term implying that you are the actual office of an airline itself, for example, "Airline Ticket Office."

STEP 3: FURNISH THE OFFICE

Too many agencies look cramped and cluttered. You want to create a totally different picture, one of professionalism and elegance, without spending a fortune. Start with at least three desks. Other than chairs, desks are your only furniture. (I do not include file cabinets as furniture.) You will use these desks for many years and will spend most of your working hours here, so you should be comfortable. But besides your own sense of comfort—which is, of course, essential—your clients should have a sense of well-being as soon as they step into your office. I cannot overstress this point.

Look in the newspaper for close-out sales of office furniture. Look at the auction listings as well. When these establishments have actually closed, they frequently auction off the remaining items at unbelievably low prices. Call up large companies and ask if they are redecorating and have desks to sell. I know of one office that obtained beautiful desks in this way. Your office will probably come with standard office carpeting, and it will do nicely until the profits start rolling in.

It is lucky for travel agents who are decorating a new office that maps are inexpensive. Sometimes very good route maps can be obtained free from the airlines. The supply of colorful brochures and posters is endless and free. For all the decor you need, just put peg boards on the wall and display your brochures.

STEP 4: INSTALL TELEPHONES

Telephones are vital to this business. A great deal of your time is spent talking to reservation agents of airlines and tour operators as well as to clients. Start simply. Have a telephone on each desk if you can afford to and have at least three numbers and a hold button. If you have fewer numbers, it is difficult for clients to reach you while you are talking to the airlines. If you are experienced in business, you might want to install a more sophisticated system from the beginning. Call the various telephone system suppliers (you will find them in the Yellow Pages) and discuss your needs.

List your agency in both the telephone book and the Yellow Pages.

STEP 5: APPOINT AN OFFICE MANAGER

If you or your partner has not had two years of full-time working experience as a travel agent, you should now hire your first employee—the office manager. If you are a travel agent and have had this experience, you can be your own office manager.

Be selective in choosing a person to manage your office. The type of manager you want depends on your own intentions toward your new business. Are you going to continue in your former work and be an absentee owner of the travel agency? If so, the office will depend totally on the manager. You will want to hire a person with a history of stability, someone who will remain with your agency for a long time. Or do you want a manager from whom you will learn the business and, when you are qualified, from whom you will take over? Select someone who has worked for a high-quality agency. You want to learn good work habits and how to match your clients' requirements with tour operators suitable for their needs.

At all times when hiring a manager be sure to select a person with good educational background and solid travel agency experience. The conferences require two years' experience. I would want five years' experience from this important employee.

Ask for references—and check them.

Find out whether he or she has ever worked for a "defaulted agency," one whose appointments have been revoked for noncompliance with conference rules. An agent who was in the employ of a defaulted agency cannot be the "qualifying entity" for your office to be approved by the conferences.

Your manager must be able to pass an examination on the material contained in the *Travel Agent's Handbook*. (This handbook is discussed later.)

Salaries vary according to area. Obtain information on appropriate salary levels from other agency owners and from local employment offices.

STEP 6: OBTAIN STATIONERY AND OTHER SUPPLIES

You must now order letterhead stationery. You will also require speed memos, quick memos, invoices, receipt books, and pads (approximately 4 by 6 inches) with the agency's name and phone number for handout information to drop-in clients. You also want the phone number on those sheets so the inquirer can call you back with booking requests. All the aforementioned items are available from business supply houses. They come in various types, and you can choose according to your taste.

We now come to an important item, the work sheets. These are also available from printers of business forms. Work sheets do not have to be letterhead since they do not leave the office. They are so important—all your clients' information will be contained on them—and so many endless types are available that I have included an illustrated example here.

Some work sheets are printed only in the front and form an envelope, which provides a folder to hold documents, invoices, confirmations, and so on. The blank back sheet is used for notes. On the single-sheet type, invoices and all the related documents are stapled to the back of the file. I believe there is less likelihood of the document being lost when it is stapled on rather than put in the envelope, but this is purely a matter of preference. It is important that work sheets have printed spaces for all the information pertaining to the reservation, both confirmations and financial positions. Order at least a thousand work sheets.

STEP 7: ORDER ESSENTIAL BOOKS

You must now order the books that are necessary in running the agency. The following is not a list of all the books you are ever likely to need; you will add others later according to the type of agency you develop.

DEPARTURE DATE		INVOICE NUMBER			AGENT			OPTION DATE	
MARCH 18 1983		3761			P.F.				MARCH 18 1983

DOE, JOHN M/M.

1	MR. JOHN DOE			ADDRESS	184 SMITH STREET	
2	MRS. JANE DOE				CLEVELAND, OHIO 44126	
3				HOME PHONE 216·392·2848		BUS. PHONE
4				BUS. NAME		
5						
6				CREDIT CARD INFO.		

PAX	FROM	TO	DATE	AIRLINE	FLIGHT	CL	LEAVE	ARRIVE	STATUS	NAME/DATE
2	CLEVELAND	JFK NEW YORK	3 18	TW	534	F	2 PM	3 58	OK	Jane TW 3/2
2	JFK NEW YORK	CLEVELAND	3 20	TW	219	F	7 20 PM	9 02 PM	OK	

PLACE/CITY	HOTELS		NITES	RATE	ACCOM.	PLAN	IN-OUT	STATUS	DATE-NAME	REMARKS
NEW YORK	PLAZA		2	$150	TWIN	E.P.	3/18-20	OK	Ellen 3/2	FULL
									Westin Hotels	Pre-pay
									Westin Hotels	to hotel

DPT./DATE	SHIP / LINE		DAYS	DECK	CABIN NO.	RATE	CAT.	STATUS	DATE	NAME

CAR RENTALS	DATE	DAYS	TYPE	STATUS	AIR·PER PERSON ADULTS		CHILDREN	FARE BREAKDOWN		
								RATE NO.		
					BASE $ 348.14				CARR	Fare Calulation
					TAX 27.86					
	NOTES				TOTAL 376.00					
TOTAL: $1,052.00					COM. 34.81					
					NET 341.19			TOTAL		

"MONIES IN"

DATE	RECEIPT NO.	TYPE OF PAYMENT	AMOUNT	Name	Ticket Numbers	Gross	Net	Comm
3/2/83	642	CHECK	$1,052.00	DOE	015 8876 331 212	376.00	341.19	34.81
				DOE	8876 331 213	376.00	344.19	34.81
		HOTEL COMMISSION	30.00					
						TOTAL	$682.38	$69.62

COMPUTATIONS — NOTES

TOTAL COMMISSION $99.62

"MONIES OUT"

DATE	PAID TO	CHECK NO.	AMOUNT PAID	FULL DEPOSIT
3/2/83	PLAZA HOTEL, N.Y.C.	888	270.00	FULL/NET

TOTAL

REFUNDS

DATE	CK. NO.	FOR	AMOUNT

Official Airline Guide (OAG)

The *Official Airline Guide* comes in two editions: North American and worldwide. These are commonly referred to in the trade as the "Domestic OAG" and the "International OAG." The domestic edition lists every domestic flight by commercial passenger airline within the United States, Canada, and the Caribbean. It is issued twice a month (twenty-four issues) and costs $146.64 a year. The international edition lists commercial passenger flights throughout the world, other than domestic flights within the United States. This edition is issued monthly (twelve issues) and costs $125.96 a year.

The two OAG editions are Bibles of the industry. They give departure and arrival times for all flights, types of aircraft used, meals served, classes of service available, and virtually any other information you might require about any specific flight.

Both the North American and worldwide editions can be ordered from

Official Airline Guide
2000 Clearwater Drive
Oak Brook, Illinois 60521

They can also be ordered by calling

- From Illinois: (800) 942–1888.
- From elsewhere in the United States: (800) 323–3537.
- From Hawaii and Alaska: (312) 654–6162.
- From Canada: (312) 654–6146.

Official Steamship Guide International

This publication is to shipping what the OAG is to airline traffic. Divided into geographical sections, it lists each shipping company and all sailings throughout the world. Very frequently used is the Caribbean cruise section, listing cruises to that area from U.S. ports. It is printed monthly, and a one-year subscription (twelve issues) costs $48. The guide can be ordered from

> Official Steamship Transportation Guides
> Subscription Department
> 111 Cherry Street, Suite 205
> New Caanan, Connecticut 06840
> Phone: (203) 227–0560

Hotel and Travel Index

Of the numerous books listing hotels, this is the one most necessary for agents. It lists hotels throughout the world, giving number of rooms, rates, and addresses. It also gives the name, address, and phone number of hotel representatives. This book is very easy to use. It is published four times per year—spring, summer, autumn, and winter—and costs $40. It can be ordered from

> Ziff-Davis Publishing Company
> Public Transportation and Travel Division
> 1 Park Avenue
> New York, New York 10016
> Phone: (212) 725–3500

Official Hotel and Resort Guide

This guide comes in three volumes in loose-leaf form and costs $155. Yearly updating service (included in the price) is available, and these changes should be inserted in the proper places. This is more of a reference book than the *Hotel and Travel Index*, giving a short description of each hotel. These volumes are especially useful when information is required on a specific hotel. It is obtainable from

International Travel Library
Post Office Box 5880
Cherry Hill, New Jersey 08034
Phone: (609) 795–7012 and (212) 725–3642

Travel Planner and Hotel/Motel Guide

This is an excellent reference book. It comes in two editions, North American and European. It has diagrams of all major airports, showing locations of all carrier terminals; city maps; and maps showing the location of hotels and motels. It also lists airport facilities for the handicapped, showing ramps, doors, and so forth. The *Travel Planner* can be ordered from the same source as the *Official Airline Guide*.

The cost of the North American edition, four issues per year, is $57.08; the European issue, also four issues per year, costs $56.80.

Any Good Atlas

You'd be surprised at the number of agencies without an atlas on the premises. But don't just buy an atlas—*use it.*

Fielding or Fodor's Guides to the Caribbean, Europe, and Other Places

Keep a reasonably up-to-date copy of either of these guides in the office. They give detailed hotel descriptions and contain a great deal of other useful information. They are available at most bookstores.

Travel 800

This little gem will save you a fortune in phone bills. It lists all airlines, shipping companies, wholesalers, hotels, car rental companies, and so on—and gives addresses and toll-free telephone numbers for them all. Don't be without this one. The cost is $10 a copy. Order from

Cadell Travel Publications
11411 Cumpson Street
North Hollywood, California 91601
Phone: (800) 854–3210; California: (800) 432–7248

The Travel Agent

This is a most useful personnel directory; it also lists foreign government offices and gives visa requirements. Published by *The Travel Agent* magazine, it costs $10 a copy.

The Travel Agent
2 West Forty-sixth Street
New York, New York 10036
Phone: (212) 575–9000

Trade Magazines

Keep current by subscribing to either

The Travel Agent
2 West Forty-sixth Street
New York, New York 10036
$7 per year

Travel Weekly
Ziff-Davis Publishing Company
1 Park Avenue
New York, New York 10016
$12 per year

Each of these magazines is published twice weekly, except for a few weeks when the number of issues varies.

For all books and periodicals listed the costs quoted include delivery.

STEP 8: SET UP BOOKING RECORDS

In order to claim retroactive commissions after your official appointments come through, you must keep accurate records of your sales. You need to keep a separate list of all domestic airline sales, international airline sales, and shipping sales. Until your appointment by the conferences, you can pick up your international airline tickets directly from the airline offices or by mail, making full payment to the airline. But you do not deduct commission at this time.

There is an important procedure for domestic bookings while awaiting appointment, and no warning is given to new agents that this is so. Retroactive commissions on ATC bookings are paid only if the ticket is obtained by using an *exchange order*. Contact all domestic carriers and ask them for exchange orders, green, envelope-type forms, since they each issue their own. When making a domestic booking, fill out the exchange order and complete both the front of the ticket envelope and the agent's copy. Enclose an agency check for the full amount of the ticket. Do not deduct commission when you are not yet appointed. Retain the agent's copy, seal the envelope, and give it to the client in place of a ticket. He or she will present it to the airline at check-in and will be given a ticket in return. You, the agent, must keep the agent's copies in your files in order to claim commission on the bookings when you have obtained your appointment. (If you prefer you can take the envelope to an airline office and obtain the ticket for your client. Remember to keep the agent's copy in your files.) At the time of appointment go through all these records and claim commissions from each carrier for your sales.

Shipping lines will mail your client's tickets to you upon receipt of full payment.

STEP 9: ADVERTISE YOUR AGENCY

Place an advertisement in the local newspaper to inform the public that your agency has opened. Both ATC and IATA expect your business to be advertised. If you have been prominent locally in business or social activities, ask the newspapers to run a story on your new business. If your office manager formerly held the same position with another agency, announce that he or she has joined your firm.

STEP 10: ORDER YOUR TICKET VALIDATOR
AND INSTALL AN OFFICE SAFE

A validator is a small machine similar to those used by stores to validate a credit card. You may order the validator while your application is pending. This ticket imprinter is for use in validating tickets after your appointment. To order your validator write to

Air Traffic Conference, Agency Department
1709 New York Avenue, N.W.
Washington, D.C. 20036
Phone: (202) 626–4000

There are two types of validators: the Addressograph Multigraph, Model 12–49, and the 867 Farrington Tolerator. The Addressograph at present costs $139; the Farrington Tolerator, $119. Either is acceptable.

Security of ticket stock is of the utmost importance, too important to be left to chance. So ATC has requirements concerning the type of safe you must install in your office. The National Bureau of Casualty Underwriters has a burglary manual that defines a "burglar resistant safe." Check directly with the bureau. The proper type of safe should have walls and floor of laminated steel. The safe should not be on rollers and it should be cemented or bolted to the floor. Make sure your safe conforms to ATC requirements.

STEP 11: APPLY FOR APPOINTMENT

This is the important step. Now that your office is open and a qualified manager is in charge, you can apply to the various conferences for appointment so that you can sell tickets and receive commissions for doing so.

Write or phone each of these conferences to ask for application forms for agency appointment:

Air Traffic Conference of America
1709 New York Avenue, N.W.
Washington, D.C. 20006
Phone: (202) 626–4000

International Air Transport Association of America
1000 Sherbrooke Street West
Montreal P.Q. H3H2R4
Phone: (514) 844–6311

International Passenger Ship Association
17 Battery Park Place
New York, New York 10004
Phone: (212) 425–7400

Pacific Cruise Conference
Suite 200
San Francisco, California 94133
Phone: (415) 981–5570

National Railroad Passenger Corporation
1 Penn Plaza
Room 1435
New York, New York 10001

Fortunately, the requirements of all these parties are almost identical, so that in preparing your records and meeting the rules of one, you are ready for all, and your appointments can be cleared as early as possible. Send the applicable fees with the application forms.

Each conference has two separate areas of requirements: (1) experience and knowledge, (2) financial ability.

The ATC will send you a bond application form (see illustration). You should complete this form with the help of your bank manager if necessary. A surety or bonding company will tell you what assets are required to obtain the bond in the amount of $10,000, which is the minimum bond required by the ATC. The amounts are based on the volume of sales and will increase as your volume grows. The maximum bond is $50,000. (A bond is required to prevent the agent from absconding with money held in trust for ATC member airlines). The ATC informs you if, or when, an increase in your bond is necessary.

Bond application forms are included in the application for authorization by IATA, IPSA, and PCC. You simply fill out these bond applications along with the other forms enclosed. These conferences, when satisfied about your financial ability, will obtain bond coverage for you. In order to obtain appointment to the conferences you should be prepared to produce the following items:

- A current financial statement from your bank. Ask your bank manager to prepare a statement showing your balances throughout the past three months.

- Sufficient working capital to defray the expenses of starting the agency and maintaining it until it is established. A working capital of $15,000 and capitalization or net worth of $20,000 are specified by IATA.

- A performance bond, as discussed, specifically in the amount of $10,000 for ATC compliance.

- Agency premises devoted exclusively to the sale of passenger transportation and related

---

Bond No. _____

AIR TRAFFIC CONFERENCE OF AMERICA
BOND FORM

KNOW ALL MEN BY THESE PRESENTS: THAT (Full Name, City & State) _____

_____

_____ (hereinafter called the Principal) and _____

_____ of _____ (hereinafter called the
Surety) are held and firmly bound unto Air Traffic Conference of America (hereinafter called the Obligee)
as agent for and in behalf of any airline member of the Obligee contracting with the Principal, in the

amount of _____ on and after the _____ day of _____.

WHEREAS, The Principal has entered into or is desirous of entering into an agreement or agreements with the Obligee known as the Sales Agency Agreement and/or Passenger Sales Agency Agreement in the form prescribed by the Obligee, which agreement is specifically incorporated herein and made a part hereof by reference;

AND WHEREAS, the Sales Agency Agreement provides, in part, that the Principal shall remit on a weekly basis for transportation sold (in accordance with said Agreement), or at such intervals as the Obligee may designate from time to time in writing, and further, that the Principal shall be entitled to deduct from such remittances the applicable commissions, as specified in said Agreement.

NOW, THEREFORE, THE CONDITION OF THIS OBLIGATION IS SUCH that if the Principal shall duly comply with the provisions of said Sales Agency Agreement with respect to remittances to the Obligee, as in said Agreement provided, then this obligation to be void, otherwise to remain in full force and effect in law, subject however to the following limitations:

1. That the Obligee shall notify the Surety of any default of the Principal hereunder, at the earliest possible time following the discovery of such default and in any event not later than 90 days after such discovery;

2. That the Surety shall promptly notify the Obligee in writing of any changes in either the Principal or amount of bond set forth above. However, failure of the Surety to provide such notice shall not affect the validity of this bond;

3. That if the Surety shall so elect; this bond may be cancelled by giving 30 days written notice to the Obligee; the Surety, however, will remain liable for any default occurring during the period up to the expiration of said *30* days notice;

4. In event of the payment by the Surety of any claims hereunder, the Surety shall be subrogated to all the rights of the Obligee with respect to such claims, and the Obligee shall execute or have executed whatever documents may be necessary in this regard;

5. That in no event shall the surety be liable for a greater amount than that shown above;

6. That the Surety shall not be subject to any suit, action or proceeding hereunder instituted later than 6 months following the termination hereof unless, prior to or within such 6 month period, the Obligee has notified the Surety of a default of the Principal hereunder.

*Signed and sealed as of the effective date mentioned above.

_____
Surety

_____
Attorney in Fact

*To be signed and sealed by an authorized representative of the Surety. If Attorney in Fact, power of attorney must be attached.

From the: *Air Traffic Conference Travel Agents Handbook.*

services. Do not forget that your agency cannot be located in a private home and must be in a business establishment easily accessible to the public.

- For the owner or office manager, three letters from former employees, business associates, customers, or other professional persons attesting to the applicant's reputation for ethical business practices, particularly in the field of passenger transportation. The letters should also show two years' experience in the sale of airline, shipping, and rail services and at least one year's experience in ticketing these services.

- Photographs of the interior and exterior of your agency. If the agency is located in an office building and does not have a street-floor entrance, a picture showing the entrance to the agency should be used.

In addition to these requirements, remember the rule, required by all conferences, that not more than 20 percent of your business can emanate from more than one source.

Agents who open businesses in Canada should not apply to the ATC for appointment. It is necessary for Canadian travel agents to file only one application for airline appointment:

International Air Transport Association of America
1000 Sherbrooke Street West
Montreal P.Q. H3H2R4
Phone: (514) 844-6311

The Canadian carriers are members of

> Air Transport Association of Canada (ATAC)
> 747 Metropolitan Life Building
> 99 Bank Street
> Ottawa KIP6B9
> Phone (613) 233–7727.

The major Canadian carriers (Air Canada and C.P. Air) are also members of IATA.

If your agency is located in an isolated area (for example, Northwest Territories) where you rely on the services of non-IATA carriers (such as Pacific Western Airlines), the carrier, who is a member of ATAC, will appoint you to sell their tickets under an "umbrella agreement" through ATAC. (You do not apply to ATAC for appointment.) You are free to sell the U.S. carriers since they are members of IATA.

An association for the travel trade is

> Alliance of Canadian Travel Associates (ACTA)
> 130 Albert Street
> Ottawa, Ontario
> Phone: (613) 238–1361

There are local branches of ACTA in each province. If you wish to join you should contact your local sector.

STEP 12: LEARN THE BUSINESS

Throughout the time these eleven steps are being implemented, start to learn the business from your office manager or partner. Ask airline representatives if their companies are giving any classes for agents. These are given less frequently by airlines now than in the past, except for TWA who maintains Breech Academy near Kansas City for training purposes. The American Society of Travel Agents (ASTA) can also provide information, and ATC conducts training classes. These courses are normally broken down into three sections: basic (reading the OAG and simple ticketing), intermediate (fares, routing, and so on), and advanced (management). Call ATC and ask where and when the classes are held and their cost. Be sure to check if food and lodging are included in the cost and if free air transportation is provided where necessary.

While your applications for appointment are pending, your office will be visited by two separate airline representatives, one representing ATC and the other IATA. Each year the conferences appoint an airline to represent them for these inspections; for example, IATA might be represented by Air France, and ATC by United Airlines. No appointment will be made for these visits. The representatives want to see your office in normal operation to be sure that it complies with all regulations. Do not fear these visits. The representatives will try to help you rather than find you at fault.

One further piece of advice about learning your business as a travel agent. *Improve your geography!* If you are going to be an agent, be a good one. Know what you are talking about. Your subject is the world, so you will never run out of material. Await your authorization—and keep learning.

6

A Big Bonus—
Travel For You

Travel agents are among the most fortunate of all people:
the world is theirs to roam.

FAMILIARIZATION TRIPS

Each year thousands of familiarization trips are offered
to travel agents by airlines, wholesalers, and government tourist offices throughout the world. These are
very inexpensive, frequently offering free air transportation. They vary from two weeks in New Zealand to a
week in Vienna. You can go on as many or as few of these
trips as you wish. The agent pays only a small charge—
which covers hotel, food, transfers, sightseeing, and
cocktail parties—and the transportation is often courtesy

of the airline. When airfare is not free, the cost is 25 percent of the normal fare.

Familiarization trips in the United States—called "domestic" trips—are available to agents on the ATC list. This is a list of full-time agency employees who have been with the agency for one complete year. These are often four-day trips, many of them including weekends. Such a trip enables the agents to see a new area without being absent from their offices for too long. It also gives them a marvelous weekend!

The purpose of familiarization trips is, as the name indicates, to become knowledgeable about a destination. It is absolutely necessary for agents to make use of these trips to learn about what they are selling. The trips are offered at incredibly low prices, and most important, they give the agents a maximum of useful information as a sound basis for advising clients intelligently. These trips always include a tour of the important hotels of the area, showing rooms in various price categories, bars, restaurants, other public rooms, and so on. Agents should always see as many hotels as possible and become familiar with what they offer. Day-long sightseeing trips are also part of the agents' tours, and they are fun and educational at the same time. (When you return do write a thank-you note to the airline who offered the trip and absorbed much of the cost.)

There is no substitute for first-hand travel. When you can give the client detailed information about accommodations in an area, you will be grateful for all the time you spent going from hotel to hotel. On such trips you build your fund of information. Use the tours, value them, learn and profit from them, and enjoy them.

As for who pays for the land and air cost, if any, on familiarization trips, each agency decides its own policy. There is also the question of whether salary should be paid to the agents while they are away from the office participating in these tours. Again, this is a matter of office policy. A profitable agency, though, which relies on good, responsible, full-time agents, would do well to absorb the costs and pay the salaries, especially if the trip is to an area the agent has not previously visited or to one used heavily by the agency's clientele. The office benefits directly by the agent's first-hand knowledge. Besides, generosity in such trips pays big dividends in employee loyalty. The office manager should see that these trips are fairly apportioned among the staff.

Every opportunity should be used to increase agents' knowledge of the travel world; it is their stock in trade. Sometimes agents feel they hardly need a home. If they wanted to they could eat out, by invitation, for breakfast, lunch, and dinner. And if the roof disappeared from over their heads—well they could always go on a familiarization trip. A tired but happy agent once confessed to me, "Sometimes I think that I know the rooms of the Intercontinental hotels around the world better than I do those in my own house!"

Agents influence a client's choice of airline, hotel, and sightseeing, at least half of the time. How can agents do this without first-hand knowledge of what they are recommending? By what authority could agents advise if they have no more knowledge of the subject than does the client's neighbor? Reliable, responsible advice can only be given where there is knowledge behind the advice. It is the agent's job to travel as much as possible and absorb information all the way.

Another good reason for actually visiting a place is that sometimes hotel brochures can be misleading, even deliberately so. For example, a photograph might show a broad expanse of beach in front of the hotel. Imagine the clients' surprise when they find a heavily trafficked road between the hotel grounds and that beach! Ah, yes, the hotel used a very good photographer, who angled the shot from far enough down the beach so that the road did not show. If your clients know beforehand exactly what to expect, they will not be disappointed, but if they expected the hotel to be directly on the beach, you will certainly hear about it.

Experienced agents who travel as often as they can, come to know the traps in the frequently used resorts. In the example of the misleading hotel brochure, no one could suspect what the situation actually was. Only personal knowledge would protect the agent.

It is a proven fact that when an agent has just visited an area, his or her sales to that area jump dramatically. Thus, the familiarization trips pay off both for the agent and for the airlines and wholesalers who have sponsored them.

DISCOUNT PASSES

There is another way to travel as an agent to any destination of your own choosing—by using discount passes.

International

In October each agency sends to IATA a list of all its qualified employees, those agents who have worked for the agency for at least a year. An agent who was previously a qualified employee of another agency may be placed on the list after working for your agency for three months, provided no more than sixty days elapsed between jobs.

Upon receipt of the list, IATA mails to the agency two discount air transportation coupons for each person on the list. These coupons are good for international transportation anywhere in the world at 75 percent discount for the entire itinerary. The coupons are known as passes, although the term "pass" is not entirely accurate since the agent pays 25 percent of the normal fee when traveling in this manner.

To use this pass the agent fills out a form stating the purpose of the trip and listing the flights; then the owner or head of the agency signs the form. The agent sends the form, the discount IATA coupon, and an agency check to cover 25 percent of the normal fare to the first airline on the itinerary. The carrier forwards the ticket or sends an official authorization for the agent to write the ticket.

Although two passes are allocated for each employee, they belong to the agency, not to the employee personally, and are normally used with the permission of the owner or the office manager. There is usually no shortage of passes, as most trips require only the IATA list to obtain complimentary air transportation.

On the agent's familiarization trips mentioned previously, whether the air transportation is free or at a 75 percent discount, a copy of the IATA list is always required when an agent wishes to go on the trip. This is to ensure that the applicant is a bona fide travel agent whose name is listed with IATA as a working member of the agency staff.

Domestic

Reduced rate transportation for domestic air trips is given on a different basis, and in most agencies, is available to fewer employees than the discount for international transportation. An agency receives two ATC passes for the first $100,000 gross of domestic sales for the past year, plus an additional pass for each additional $100,000 or fraction thereof. Again "pass" means a 75 percent discount on the regular fare.

OTHER DISCOUNTS

If you are traveling other than on an agent's trip, hotels normally offer you a discount on the room, anywhere from 25 to 50 percent. Simply send a letter to the hotel manager on your agency letterhead stationery, giving the dates you intend to be there, and ask if an agent's discount can be granted. Enclose your business card.

Cruise ships and shipping lines in general offer agent's discounts. These vary according to the line concerned and how heavily the particular cruise is booked. The lines generally extend the discount privilege to a spouse and children when they are traveling with an agent, but there is no set rule. Write to the shipping line concerned and state your requirements. If the ship is not heavily booked, you are likely to receive a generous discount. Your shipping line representatives will discuss with you which particular sailings are not heavily booked and are therefore most likely to afford discounts.

ACTIVE SOCIAL LIFE

Travel and pleasant work is not the only benefit offered to the agent. Indeed the travel agent need never have a dull social life. There is a constant flow of cocktail parties given by airlines and tourist offices to promote their offerings for the coming season. These parties, usually given in hotels in cities and suburbs, begin with cocktails and hors d'oeuvres, followed by a film presentation and talk regarding new fares, tours, and package offerings for the public. Brochures are amply available for the agents to bring back to their offices.

Also, wholesalers give breakfast and luncheon presentations of their new packages. Again, the event is held at a hotel, and after the meal a talk or a film show is given to explain the new product. These events are an enjoyable way for agents to keep up with new developments and also to have a chance to socialize and compare notes and business. Agency personnel should be encouraged to attend as many of these social familiarization programs as they can.

7

Your Working Associates

After you have completed your applications for a travel agent's appointment you cannot sit back and wait for accreditation. You are going to be dealing with the travel industry as a whole, not just with the conferences. You will find quite a collection of fellow workers in the various branches of the industry: airline reservation services, shipping reservations, airlines and shipping lines, hotels, tours, and car rental companies. Because you will deal with these people constantly, we will look at what they do and how they affect your job.

TELEPHONE RESERVATIONS STAFF

All travel services employ telephone reservation agents whose job is to receive requests for service and give confirmations as available. These people are known in the industry as "res agents". A great deal of your day is spent talking to them, especially those with airlines. You will have a toll-free number for a reservation agent who handles only travel agents' business. These agents have a tiring and responsible job. They work all day with telephones and computers, trying to match your requests with available space. The res staff is human, so patience and cooperation on your part will get willing service and special attention when you need it. Don't make a fuss if you are left on hold longer than you want. You are using an 800 (toll-free) number, and you are on hold because the res agent is searching for an acceptable alternate if your first request cannot be filled.

AIRLINE REPRESENTATIVES

Always known as "airline reps," their job is to represent their airline with all the travel agents within a specified area. They bring promotional material and advise you of new fares. Their job is to increase their airline's share of your business. Reps spend four out of five working days each week calling on agents. The other day (often Mondays) they can be found in their offices in the airline's administrative building. When possible choose that day to telephone them. On other days, when they are out on calls, they check back with their office for messages and will return your calls as quickly as possible. On their day in the office they will usually attend an airline sales meeting, where the airline's volume of sales on its various routes is discussed. If one route is doing poorly, pressure will be put on the reps to increase production there. They, in turn, will come to your office and ask you specifically to give them business on the route in question. Help them when you can. Good rapport with airline reps is important for your business, and mutual support is to the advantage of both the airline and the agent, and consequently, of the client.

Airline reps are the people to call about problems and complaints. It is a good idea to keep a manila folder for each airline. When you have a problem with a particular airline, make a note of it and toss it into the appropriate folder. Before reps leave your office, glance at the folder for their airline, and if a problem exists, ask for their help. Reps can also help you find seats when space is very tight, as on Christmas flights to Florida. But don't turn to the reps every time a flight is sold out. Save this favor for a really important matter. Especially do not ask favors for clients who are in the habit of canceling at the last moment. Your reps will come through whenever humanly possible if they know you do not abuse the privilege. Reps often become good friends of the agent. They can suggest successful promotional ideas, and they can even see shortcomings in your office that are not apparent to you.

SHIPPING LINE REPRESENTATIVES

These reps perform exactly the same service for shipping and cruise lines as the airline reps do for the airlines.

WHOLESALERS OR TOUR OPERATORS

This segment of the industry occupies as definite a place as the travel agencies. Like travel agents, wholesalers sell the services of the airlines and hotels, and like airline personnel, they rely on the travel agent to supply them with the majority of their clients. Tour operators have less direct contact with the client than does the agent. They occasionally send representatives to call on agents, but they are not as regular visitors as the airline or shipping reps. It is possible and permissible for a client to book a tour with a wholesaler, but it is much more usual for a travel agent to be the intermediary. Many established tour operators belong to the U.S. Tour Operator's Association, and as such, are required to post a $100,000 bond to cover any losses incurred by the travel agent. An acceptable alternative is a tour operator's participation in ASTA's Tour Payment Protection Plan, formed in March 1982. It requires participating tour operators to leave on deposit a security of $100,000 or $50,000, depending on the company's sales volume.

Tour packages can take various forms. The component parts are transportation, hotel reservations, meals, intercity touring, sightseeing, car rental, and partial or full escort service for groups. Any of these services can be combined to form a package. The emphasis varies according to the tour operator, from the lowest priced cost-conscious tour to the deluxe. Tours are available for all tastes: expeditions to study the biology of the Galapagos or the mythology of Greece; specials for sportspersons and spectators; gambling junkets; or the usual package of transportation, hotel, and sightseeing.

Wholesalers buy hotel space in bulk, and because of that volume, receive a lower rate than an individual traveler. Frequently a group rate can be obtained for air travel also. Tour operators make a deposit payment on all guaranteed space and depend on business from travel agencies to make their final payment and give them a profit. Agents are careful to choose reliable wholesalers since their clients' money, as well as their enjoyment, is in the wholesaler's hands. It is advisable to use tour operators who have affiliated themselves with the U.S.

Tour Operators Association or ASTA Tour Payment Protection Plan. This requirement assures the safety of your client's payments, and thus protects you from possible lawsuits should the tour operator fail to perform the promised services.

HOTEL RESERVATION SERVICES

There are two types of reservation services: those run by hotels themselves and those run by a hotel representative serving many hotels.

Hotel's Own Service

Hotel chains have 800 telephone numbers for agents to call the chain's reservation staff, just as agents call the airline's reservation service. Some individual hotels also have this service.

Hotel Representatives

This is a business in itself. Hotel representatives have a list of hotels whom they represent and for whom they act as a reservation service. Major foreign hotels are all represented in this manner, so that securing reservations becomes a simple matter and no overseas phone calls or letter writing is needed. Utell International, Robert Warner, and Robert Reid Associates are examples of U.S. hotel representatives. The hotel reps should be familiar with every property they handle and should be able to answer all your questions regarding facilities. They will either give you instant confirmation or get back to you very quickly on the status of the rooms requested. When all hotels in a particular area are sold out, the hotel rep usually knows the reason—a convention or a major trade fair, perhaps —and can suggest the nearest alternative.

CAR RENTAL AGENTS

All car rental services have their own telephone reservation system of toll-free numbers. The reservation agents will offer the various types of car rentals available and describe costs, insurance, and any particular packages. They can give you immediate confirmation of any type of car for hire in either the domestic or the international market.

OTHER AGENTS IN YOUR AREA

It is always wise to get to know others in the same line of work. They have the same interests as you do and the same problems. They can provide advice and shop talk, and even actual assistance.

Remember that in the period before obtaining appointment you are working without income from the airlines and shipping companies. If this proves to be too great a burden, an already appointed agent can help you out. Instead of getting the international airline ticket from the airlines and issuing the exchange orders to your domestic airline clients, you can make an arrangement with another agency to write airline tickets that you can pick up and give to your clients. You can split the commission with the issuing agent, usually 50–50, or in any ratio agreeable to both agents. For convenience, choose an agency located near your office. This arrangement is perfectly legal. Do be aware, however, that if you follow this arrangement a great deal, it becomes difficult to show productivity to the airlines, since the issuing agent is being credited with the booking.

If you need income, use the method of split commission within reason. (But do deal directly with the airlines frequently enough to show them that you will be an asset to them as an appointed agent.) All airlines look for sales volume on their own service. They know that your volume will not be large when your agency is newly opened, but they do expect some bookings, especially the major trunk carriers. If an agent never books a particular carrier, the carrier concludes that it is not worth the expense of being represented by that agency.

YOUR BROCHURE COLLECTION

You have now met the suppliers of the product you will sell. This is the time to ask for brochures and to establish reference files. If you have a back office, it is an ideal place for these file cabinets. Label file drawers by area: Europe, Caribbean, Africa. Use cardboard subdividers and section each area alphabetically by country. Ask hotel reps for brochures of hotels they represent, and file materials according to area. Airlines and tour operators will send brochures on their package deals; file them by area too. Just call your travel associates, and they'll start the flow!

8

Getting Into Your Travel Business

Congratulations—your ATC appointment has been confirmed, followed shortly by IATA authorization. The shipping lines' approval will arrive a little later. Now you no longer have to run around to get tickets. Your name will be placed on the ATC official agency list, and ATC will give you an agency code number, which is also your official IATA number. It is used to identify your agency to the airlines and conferences for reservations, ticketing, and reporting airline sales.

Upon appointment, you receive from ATC three items: an agency identification plate, an agent passenger ticket requisition form, and the *Travel Agents Handbook*.

AGENCY IDENTIFICATION PLATE

This is a small metal plate approximately 1 inch by ½ inch on which is imprinted your agency's name, location, and number. It is placed in your validator to validate all airline tickets.

In addition to your agency plate, you need another plate to complete the validation of an airline ticket—the identification plate of the airline concerned. This plate, also metal, shows the name of the airline, its emblem, and its code number (see illustration).

The airlines are informed by ATC and IATA of your appointment to the official list of agents. The carriers who choose you to sell their tickets will either send you

AIRLINE PLATE

PROPERTY OF FLYRIGHT AIRWAYS

>>> FLYRIGHT
222

222

AGENCY PLATE

ABC TRAVEL INC.

PITTSBURG, PA

22   34567   8A

their airline validation plate or have their representative for your area call at your office to bring it to you. It is fun at this stage to get an airline validation plate holder and watch it fill up with authorization plates.

It is not mandatory, however, for an airline to authorize you to represent it, even though ATC and IATA have approved you. If you have had no sales for a particular carrier while waiting for appointment, that carrier might decide that you would be a nonproductive agent. You have to convince the carrier that should it choose to let you sell its tickets, you can provide sales. If an airline has not chosen you to represent it, whenever possible book your clients on another carrier flying the same route. Let some time elapse; then call the representative for the airline withholding appointment and ask him or her to reconsider. Explain that you have potential bookings for that airline, relating your good sales record with other carriers. Approval will not be long delayed.

AGENCY PASSENGER TICKET REQUISITION FORM

This form lists all the available types of airline tickets, travel documents, and administrative forms. (Travel documents include all official ATC forms agents use for airline reservations—tickets, ticket refund notices, tour orders, and miscellaneous charge orders.) You simply state how many of each type of document you require. The first time you use this form, you should ask your office manager for advice.

Tickets are issued by ATC to agencies in blocks. You may order on your ticket requisition form approximately three months' supplies. No more than approximately two days' usage of tickets should be retained in the office, and these must be locked in the steel safe when the office is not staffed. The remaining portion of your ticket orders should be kept in a bank safety deposit box. If no bank is near you, you may use a safety deposit box in a hotel.

A definite responsibility is attached to owning ticket stock, your agency validation plate, and airlines' validation plates. Any ticket validated with your agency plate is the responsibility of your agency.

Tickets have serial numbers at the top right-hand corner and must be used in sequence. No ticket, even if written incorrectly, can be thrown away. All tickets and numbered administrative forms must be accounted for in a weekly sales report. A safety measure that can spare you a great deal of anguish is keeping a ledger for ticket control. Keep a separate section or few pages of the ledger for each type of flight ticket and each type of numbered adminstrative form. Head each page in this way:

TICKET NUMBER	CLIENT NAME	DATE	FORM OF PAY-MENT	ISSUED BY (Em-ployee)

Fill out this page each time a ticket or other official document is written. Then any missing ticket can easily be checked.

Each evening, when you close the agency, you must lock in your safe the agency plate, folder of all the airline plates, and ticket stock kept in the agency.

TRAVEL AGENTS HANDBOOK

This manual describes every form of ticket and travel document and also illustrates in detail how to write and use them. The book cannot substitute for classes in how to write tickets, but it is an excellent and comprehensive reference manual and should be kept in your office at all times. It is, however, written in "legalese" style and could be difficult to follow if you are not already familiar with agency procedures. It contains the ATC Sales Agency Agreement, which spells out the rules governing agencies and the obligation of agents. If you are ever in doubt about a technical or procedural matter, you can most likely find the answer in the *Travel Agents Handbook.*

WORK SHEETS AND FILES

The essential component of your files is the work sheet. You know how to take care of the completed forms, and you have seen an example of a completed work sheet (Chapter 5, pages 54–55). These work sheets must be filled out properly.

When your client walks into your office, you will reach for your pad of work sheets. Use one work sheet for each trip, whether one or more people are traveling together. List all the passengers' names on the file. Note on the work sheet all the services the client requires— airline reservations, car rentals, hotels, and so on. You will sit with the work sheet in front of you when you talk to various reservation staffs. Start with flight availability. Then if the client is picking up a car at the airport, the car rental agent can be told the client's incoming flight number. Note on the work sheet the date of confirmation and the name of the confirming agent for each service you call. Hotel and car reservation services may give a confirmation number in place of the agents' name.

Always fill in fully

- Client's name, address, and work and home telephone numbers.
- Flight itinerary, whether confirmed, name of confirming agent, date confirmed.
- Hotel reservations: city, hotel, type of room, occupancy dates, costs, date confirmed, reservation number or name of confirming agent.
- Car rental: city, type of car, dates of hire, costs, conditions of rental (what is included—mileage, insurance), confirmation number.
- Shipping reservation: name of ship, shipping line, date of sailing, cabin number, cost per person, option date, name of reservation agent, date requested, date confirmed.

Worksheets should also show the breakdown of airfare on the front of the sheet and the total cost of all reservations. Departure dates should be placed on the top of the right-hand side where, along with the client's name, they can be read in the file drawer.

The back of the file should show receipt and invoice numbers, ticket numbers, date ticketed, total cost of the ticket, and amount of commission. All payments made by clients to the agency must be noted on the back of the file, as well as all payments, and payment date, made by the agent to suppliers on behalf of the client.

The numbers of any and all credit cards the customer is using for payment must be noted on the file as well as the kinds of cards, expiration dates, name of client as noted on the cards, and business name on any card issued to a business.

Commissions due (from hotels, car rentals, and so on) will also be listed on this section of the file. They will be sent to you after the client's trip is over.

It is vitally important that every member of the staff fills out the worksheets in an identical manner, and that complete information pertaining to the clients and their trips and all financial details are noted. Any person on the staff should be able to pick up any office file and know exactly which reservations are confirmed and what is paid for and be able to answer any question pertaining to the booking. This is an absolute must. Your entire business is contained in these files.

FILING SYSTEM

There are many methods of filing work sheets. I believe that the safest way is to file by date. When you set up your office, divide an entire file drawer into twelve sections, one for each month of the year. Use cardboard file dividers and print the month on the file tab. Place the current month at the front of the file and work backward in order. Then, to file by date, just place the work sheet in the month of the client's departure. File chronologically within each month—the first at the front of the drawer, the thirtieth at the back.

At times, however, you will be given a specific date by which time a deposit, such as a hotel deposit, must be received. This is known as an *option date*. Let's say that your client plans to depart on June 6, but the hotel deposit must be made on May 4. The whole folder will be filed under May 4, with a small square of paper marked "hotel deposit May 4" clipped to it. Using this method, you will not miss an option date. If one were missed, the reservation would be lost—which is not likely to result in a happy client.

The drawer with the files waiting for options or ticketing by a certain date is called the *active file*—clients who have not yet departed. In the file drawer below this active file, set up two sections: complete and incomplete. Divide each section into twelve sections, one for each month. At the end of a month remove all the folders filed under that month from the active file to the lower drawer. When no commission is due, file the folder chronologically in the "complete" section. However, if a commission is due, place the folder in the "incomplete" section under the appropriate month (the month of the client's departure). In this manner of filing, no commissions owed to the agency are overlooked.

With these guiding principles your office will run smoothly.

Now you have information on how to fill out and file the work sheets. You will have learned in class how to write and issue tickets, and you know enough not to let any ticket leave the office without payment (with the possible exception of commercial accounts, which we discuss later in this book).

THE AGENCY SALES REPORT

Now we have come to an extremely important matter. You are holding a great deal of money that actually belongs to the airlines. You will keep your commissions, but the money belonging to the airlines must be paid. You do this every week in the form of the agency sales report.

To prepare your report, check all airline tickets and official documents sold during the past week from Monday morning to Sunday evening. Put each type of ticket and related document in sequence and be sure that none is missing.

The method of writing this report, as well as writing airline tickets, will be taught to you in class. The *Travel Agents Handbook* also explains in detail how to make out a sales report. It is not difficult. Essentially you add all your cash sales on an adding maching tape, add all the credit card sales on a separate tape (fifty per tape; continue on new tape), compute the total, deduct the commissions, and fill out the authorization section of the form. Attach to the report an auditor's coupon (contained in each document) of each ticket or other document used, and send the report to the ATC area bank designated by ATC. No check is enclosed. The report is your authorization to ATC to withdraw the amount from your bank.

Write your report at the same time each week (Monday morning is a good time), so that it can *never* be overlooked, and *never, never* let it be possible that payment funds are not available in your bank. *Your report and the bank account to support it must always be in order.* Be sure the report for the previous week is mailed to reach the area bank by the close of banking hours on Tuesday of each week. Mail on Monday. If there is any doubt that the report will arrive in time, get a stamped certificate of mailing from the post office. Should you have no sales for any reporting period, you must file a report to that effect. Keep a duplicate copy of each sales report with copies of supporting documents for at least two years.

Penalties for noncompliance with the reporting rules are very strict. According to *Travel Agents Handbook*, if a check is dishonored,

- ATC informs the bonding company, IATA, and all airlines.

- The agent must provide a certified check to cover the dishonored check.

- Each dishonored check will count as three late remittance notices (which is likely to lead to an audit by ATC).

- If the agent cannot supply a certified check in the amount due, all ticket stock and airline pla'es will be removed.

- If tne amount due is not paid within thirty days, the agency is terminated and removed from the ATC agency list. The agent can appeal.

Similar penalties are levied should the agent fail to file a report for any weekly period of sales. Records are made of agency delinquencies, and copies are sent to the airlines. If an agent appears on such a record six times within a twelve-month period, he or she will be reviewed by the travel agent commissioner.

Should the agency sales report authorize an insufficient amount of money to cover the amount of sales, the area bank bills the agent for the shortage. If this amount is not settled within ten days, it is treated as a dishonored check. If it occurs frequently the agent is reviewed by the travel agent commissioner, with the possibility that ticket stock and airline plates will be removed and even that the agency will be terminated.

These are strict measures but understandable as an effort to prevent an unscrupulous agent from absconding with large amounts of money belonging to airlines.

Compliance with these rules keeps your agency in good standing, and observance of the following guidelines should keep it running smoothly:

- Develop the habit of writing "tickets to be picked up" for the day first thing in the morning when you come into the office. At that time the office is quiet. Tickets should be completed and ready to hand over when the customer comes in, because at this time your office might well resemble an expressway at rush hour. Your client then has to wait while you write the tickets, and other customers are also waiting to be taken care of. I can tell you from experience that this is when errors occur. When you feel pressured, you try to hurry, and you can make mistakes even with simple tickets.

   Also, most clients like to chat with you as you write the tickets, which can be disastrous. It's hard to keep your mind on American Airlines, Flight 021, when the voice on the other side of the desk is telling you about the last time she flew to California. It is more professional to have everything prepared when you have advance notice that a client will be in.

   Many times of course a client will walk in, state a request, and want a ticket right away. In this case, simply do the job while he or she sits at your desk. Be pleasantly friendly, but do not encourage conversation while you write the ticket.

- Deposit all checks and cash daily in your bank.

- Fill out all work sheets fully and accurately.

- File work sheets properly by date.

- Use 800 or other toll-free telephone numbers

at all times. Where there is no 800 or enterprise number, call by reversing charges to wholesalers, hotel representatives, and airlines. Never, of course, call your client by reversing charges. Insist that each employee follows the rule. Huge telephone bills are avoidable.

- Order at least one trade paper—*Travel Weekly* or *The Travel Agent.* Keep current with events, especially upcoming fare changes, so that tickets can be paid and written before fares increase.

- Join a travel agents' association. Membership in these groups frequently entitles you to increased commissions with wholesalers, shipping companies, car rental companies and others.

- Build up override commissions (explained in the following chapter). Most wholesalers pay increased commission rates after a given number of passenger bookings. Therefore, when it is suitable for your clients, sell the same wholesaler repeatedly to build up your volume and obtain the extra commissions.

- Draw up a waiver or disclaimer form. This should be a short form to be signed by all clients booked on tours arranged by wholesalers or on charter air services (see illustration).

CHARTER AIR SERVICES

Most charter companies are reputable. Unfortunately, the charter market, competitive and volatile at best, attracts some operators whose credentials are less than satisfactory. You need to know a little of the background of the charter market to understand this situation.

A charter means that a company has hired an aircraft for a specific flight. The company sets its own fares for the sales of seats, and these fares are substantially lower than the fares charged by scheduled airliners for the same service. Charters arrive at their fares per passenger by taking the cost of the plane as a base figure. This fare is divided by the number of seats on the plane, which gives the cost per person of hiring the plane. To this figure a profit is added per head, and the total will be the fare charged for each passenger.

It is obvious that the low fares for charters are based on the sale of every seat. Should the company be unable to sell all the seats, they might either cancel the charter or alter the departure date so that two flights, each of which were lagging in sales, can be amalgamated. Last-minute alteration of dates can upset your clients' hotel and tour plans at the destination, as well as leaving them liable for cancellation fees. Delays in departure are frequent on charter flights. The rights of scheduled aircraft precede the rights of charters at all times, other than emergencies.

Because the profit margin is low, difficulties can arise easily in charter companies. When airlines set low excursion fares, charters become less attractive to the public. At this point the companies become difficult to reach by phone, and it is very hard to solve any problems you may have.

Why, then, would you consider selling this market? The charter companies advertise heavily, and their prices can be low. The public is very price conscious. There is a psychological factor here too: "If it's in the newspapers it must be all right." Once the clients read that the flight, hotel, and extras are all included for, say,

EXAMPLE OF WAIVER FORM:

ABC TRAVEL SERVICE
107 TRAVELLERS LANE
SAN ANTONIO, TEXAS

We have supplied you with brochures explaining conditions and cancellation penalties of the tour, cruise, charter flights on which we have confirmed space for you. You have read and fully understood this brochure and accept that

_____ Tour Operator
_____ Cruise Line
_____ Charter Air
_____ Hotel

are solely responsible for fulfilling the conditions of this tour. ABC Travel Service is responsible only for securing space for you on the tour.

Agreed to and signed: _____
                 Date: _____
Document received: _____
                 Date: _____

$500, it is not easy for them to accept the figure of $950 on a scheduled airline, for what seems to be the same product. If you decide against selling charters, you automatically close the door to clients with a limited budget or those who prefer to take more, but less expensive, vacations per year.

The stress of being responsible for the sale of chartered space can be great. The ability to solve problems is out of your hands—that in itself is stressful. If you think your peace of mind is more important than coping with this area of the market, simply do not sell charters. Many agents do not. Decide for yourself. If you do decide to sell charters, be sure the waiver form is signed and dated by your client (see page 98). The essential point of a waiver form is to make it clear to the clients that they are using charter air or wholesaler space of which the agent is not in control, that they have read the conditions and the rules and fully understand the risks they are taking, and that they are willing to assume those risks without holding the agency responsible.

9

Handling Your Agency's Money

Most people realize that agencies earn their income from commissions, and they generally believe that agencies survive almost entirely on commissions from the sale of airline tickets. Is this true?

The following list shows the commissions a travel agent receives from various kinds of business and what percentage of the total agency market each service represents (the latter is from the Louis Harris survey in *Travel Weekly*).

Service	Percentage Commission Paid	Percentage of Agency Market
Domestic air	10	63
International air	8–11	

Service	Percentage Commission Paid	Percentage of Agency Market
Cruises	10 (frequently 12–15 for members of association)	13
Hotel	10 (international sometimes 8); frequently higher on special offerings to association members)	10
Car rental	10	7
Rail	10	3
Tours	10–15	
Sightseeing	10	4
Transfers	10	
Travel insurance	33–35	

Although the percentage of airline sales is high for most agencies, you can see that substantial fees are also paid by other kinds of travel markets. Your objective, in each transaction, is to include as many elements as possible so you can get commissions from each supplier. Let us look more closely at the commissions.

Commissions for airline travel are clear-cut. Domestic air service pays a straight 10 percent commission. International airline bookings pay 8 percent commission unless other services are sold in conjunction. When you book a complete tour, you will earn not only 10 percent commission on the tour package but also 11 percent on the air fare. Tours have official identity numbers. The airline ticket to be used in conjunction with the tour should show the tour number, which entitles you to the increased airline commission. (Domestic air commission is 10 percent with or without a tour, but put the identity number on the airline ticket if a tour is involved.)

If the passenger is not booked on a tour but requires hotel and two other related services (such as meals and sightseeing), and if these services are prepaid, you can book the land portion through a wholesaler and get a tour number entitling you to the increased air commission. It is illegal to add the tour number to a ticket without prepayment of hotel and two other related services.

You will notice that cruises, tours, and hotels pay a variable scale of commission. There are two ways to obtain the higher commissions for these services.

1. *Override*. Override is an increased percentage of commission paid after certain levels of productivity have been achieved: a base commission is 10 percent; after twenty-five bookings, 12.5 percent; after thirty-five bookings, 15 percent.

Override commissions can be retroactive. On reaching thirty-five bookings, you would then call the supplier and request the additional commissions for the previous thirty-four reservations.

To build up override, choose a wholesaler or cruise ship line that can serve the largest section of your clientele and book it as frequently as possible. (Note: never compromise any client's best interest for this end; individual service to each client comes first.) Read the trade magazines for information about which wholesalers, cruise ships, and hotels are offering override commissions at certain periods.

2. *Consortium*. Suppliers offer members of various travel associations increased commissions for specific reservations. TravelSavers is an example. When you join

one of these groups you are given a rubber stamp with its name or logo. Mention your membership when you make a reservation, and stamp your invoice and any other documents with the identifying mark when you send in the deposit. This step establishes from the start that you will receive the agreed-on increase in commission.

In Chapter 14, "Building Up the Business," we discuss the technique of selling as comprehensively as possible. When asked for flight reservations, inquire about hotels, car rentals, and insurance. How is the client getting from home to the airport? If he or she is not driving, you can get 10 percent from the local airport limousine service or set up your own commission arrangement with a driver who operates a private car service. You can become a good source of business for the driver, and thus you are in a position to negotiate an advantageous fee.

COMMISSION PAYMENTS

For airline tickets, commissions are available immediately. They are deducted from your weekly payment to the airlines by means of the sales report. For cash sales withhold the commission, and for credit card sales subtract the commission from the total due.

For shipping lines and wholesalers, after the reservation is made, a deposit must be forwarded within a few days to hold the reservation. An option date is established for final payment, approximately four to six weeks before departure. At the time of forwarding final payment deduct your commission. You are therefore paid before the client departs.

There are various methods of paying hotels and receiving your commission. First, full prepayment can be made and the commission deducted. Second, if the client does not want to prepay the entire stay, a deposit (usually one night) is forwarded but no commission deducted. You will have to wait until the client completes the hotel stay and pays the balance due. The hotel will then forward your commission by check. In each case the hotel reservation agent will tell you whether to send payment or deposit to the agent or directly to the hotel. Third, if the client is using a credit card to guarantee the room and make the hotel payment, give the credit card particulars to the hotel representative. The client completes the hotel stay and uses the credit card for payment. After being paid by the credit card company, the hotel forwards your commission check.

Advance cash payment is not made to car rental companies except occasionally for particular packages. If the rental company requires any guarantee, it is given in the form of the client's credit card number. Commission payment is made by check after the car is returned to the rental company and the fees collected.

Whenever possible deduct your commissions from your payments to the supplier. This will avoid waiting for the commission to be sent and perhaps having to write letters requesting payment. Commissions outstanding can be a major problem, especially when dealing with services overseas. A commission sent by a foreign supplier will be a check in foreign funds. You will encounter delay in cashing the check, you will be charged a bank fee, and you will be unlikely to be given a favorable exchange rate by the supplier or the bank. So where possible—deduct.

Payment vouchers can be used for hotel and car prepayment or deposits, or even simply for confirmation. Various travel associations print payment vouchers, for example, ASTA and TravelSavers. The details of the reservation are typed into the voucher and a copy is given to the client. On the agent's and supplier's copies, commission details are also spelled out. Send the supplier's copy to the hotel or rental company, and attach the agent's copy to the file. Hertz and Avis also issue their own vouchers to agents, the use of which makes commission deductions simple.

ACCOUNTING METHODS

While you are establishing your agency you should be looking for the simplest form of accounting that will work efficiently. Too many agencies are bogged down by complicated accounting systems. It should not take the agent longer to record the financial side of the sale then it took to make the reservation. Do not burden your agency with a cumbersome financial system that absorbs too much of the employee's time.

When a client comes into your office, makes a reservation, and pays with either cash or check, you should follow well-defined steps, such as the following:

- When the check is an amount of $100 or over, check with the bank on which it is issued to see that it is valid.

- Write a receipt. A simple receipt book providing one duplicate will do. Give the client the original receipt; leave the duplicate in the receipt book.

- Type an invoice in triplicate. Invoices should be numbered in sequence. The original goes to the client, the first copy is attached to the

file, and the second copy is put in the drawer
marked "invoices," filed in sequence. Triplicate invoice sheets are in three colors to facilitate filing.

When the client pays by credit card, no cash receipt is
needed. Simply issue the invoice.

At the end of each business day, take out the cash
receipt book and total the cash payments and the payments by check. Then total the cash and checks that are
in the safe. The two sums should tally. The advantage of
doing this task daily is that should any discrepency arise,
you can review the day and possibly recall what might
have caused the problem. Keep a small notebook to
record the daily bank deposits, for example:

Date	Receipts	Total
July 16	237–254	$4,321

It is easy, then, at any given time to look at the receipt
book and check each day's deposit.

At the outset of your business you will not have
reserve funds. Your deposits will go straight into the
checking account to ensure that funds are available to
meet the weekly ATC sales draft. As your business ex-
pands, and your account becomes established in the
bank, talk to the bank manager. If you open a savings
account to hold money not required for the sales report,
will he or she guarantee to move funds to your checking
account if it should at any time be short? Also have an
agreement *never* to let the report check bounce. Make
sure that when the manager is on vacation the matter is
taken care of by someone else.

OUTGOING PAYMENTS

You must make outgoing payments in time to meet option dates. The date of payment, to whom it is made, and the amount paid should be listed on the back of the file. The checkbook stub should also show the amount of payment, to whom it is made, and the client's name, and it should be marked either *deposit* or *final payment*. In this way you can have a cross-reference for accuracy.

In any business the policy is to bring in as much cash as early in the transaction as possible and to make outgoing payments in time to meet deadlines, but not earlier. In times of high interest rates it is especially important to retain money in your bank account as long as possible.

In the travel business there are only certain times when you can take advantage of cash flow by being paid ahead of option deadlines. When airline reservations are requested close to the departure date, obviously the ticket is paid for, written, and reported (therefore paid for by the agent to the airline) within days. Most business travel falls into this category.

The vacation brochures that tour operators prepare for clients spell out precisely the payment requirements: a deposit at time of booking and final payment four to six weeks before departure. In this situation the clients will not want to part with their money ahead of the stated times and the amounts, as they too want to earn bank interest as long as possible.

You must ask for substantial deposits for individually tailored itineraries. And it is both fair and necessary to do so. You will devote a good deal of time to choosing hotels and planning these trips, and a sizable deposit should be made (such as fifty dollars per person) before you begin this work to guarantee your clients' dependability. Hotel deposits will follow. In group work this requirement is vitally important and provides you with valuable cash flow.

FINANCIAL RECORDS

Every owner or manager should know the annual volume of business generated by the agency. This information is always available to you if you have an organized system of recording sales.

We discussed the importance of a "full information" file from the point of view of reservations and confirmations. It is equally important from the financial standpoint. Every file shows a breakdown of the cost of the trip: flight or ship, hotels, car rentals, tours, and the total cost of the booking. These costs are entered on the file when they are quoted to you by the reservation agent; the date and amount of payents by a client to you, and by you to the supplier, are also listed on the file.

To record these data, buy a wide ledger and make column headings such as these:

Departure Date	Invoice Number	Intern'l Air	Domestic Air	Tours	Hotels	Car Rental	Total Sale

After the client's departure date, move the file to the drawer under the active file (see page 92). Then file it in the complete or incomplete section according to whether the commission is due. When you move the file, enter in the ledger the various gross sales under the appropriate heading. You then have, automatically, a month-by-month breakdown of the type of your sales and the total amount. You can easily make comparisons from one month to another and one year to another. You then know the type of service you are selling heavily and where your sales are low. Give the facing page of the ledger similar headings, and enter the *commission amounts* for each service. Now you also have a breakdown of your profits. This is a simple system and it shows clearly your volume and profits for each service for any given period.

Records are important. Set them up from the beginning and keep them accurate and up to date.

Each airline has a record of the volume of business it receives annually from each agency. The representatives will give you this information for your own agency.

PROFITABILITY

It is simple to ascertain whether you are making money. By recording the total commissions for any period, you have already accounted for the payments to travel suppliers; the commissions are amounts belonging to the agent after the suppliers are paid. But you still have expenses to meet: salaries, rent, utilities, office supplies, perhaps computer rental. These are fixed expenses that do not vary month to month. (Utilities vary with the season and phone bills with volume of business, but average figures for them can be calculated.) The total fixed expenses should be added together and subtracted from the total commissions. You then know your actual profit. These figures are important considerations in estimating the value of your agency. They also indicate to you whether your method of running the agency is sound.

To curtail expenses you should pay attention to the following:

- Be absolutely sure that toll-free telephone numbers, or even reverse calls where indicated, are used at all times when calling suppliers. Never allow employees to disregard this rule. Go over your telephone bills to find where your heaviest expenses lie. Consult various telephone companies to see whether you could save money and get better service with a different system.

- Keep an eye on "marginal" commerical accounts. (Commercial accounts are discussed in Chapter 13.) In accounts where the majority of flights involve short distances, where changes in itinerary occur frequently, where payment is not made upon delivery of the ticket, you must decide whether the profit is in proportion to the time spent.

- Where possible use advertising for which the supplier picks up a portion of the costs; cruise lines are generous about that. A local newspaper chain may service a large area. Pool advertising costs with other agents in the same general area, but not in your immediate neighborhood. That way costs can be split among several agencies, with each reaping rewards in its particular area.

- Bill your clients well ahead of option dates.

- Be sure the client has paid you before you pay the supplier.

- Follow up on all commissions due. Have one agent review the incomplete files every month for commissions still outstanding. If you have trouble collecting a hotel commission (overseas hotels can be slow in forwarding commissions), call the hotel representative. Representatives will expect you to have written several letters to the hotel before you contact them, but at this point they will step in and help you.

- If you still don't get paid, inform ASTA, whether or not you are a member. This organization serves as a protection for agencies. If ASTA receives consistent complaints regarding any supplier, it will warn agents, and in order to survive, the supplier is likely to change its attitude and pay up.

- At the end of every year review the year's financial figures—volume in each area, commissions, expenses. Note increases or decreases in volume of total business and profits. Compare them with previous years. If any large, one-time event affected your final figure—for example, if you refurnished the entire office—you should make a note of this on the record. You would probably want this information in future years when you are checking back.

When your agency outgrows simple bookkeeping procedures, have your accountant set up a more sophisticated system. It would be wise to discuss computerized accounting then too, even if that step is still in the future for your office.

10

Your Staff— How To Choose Them

Your staff *is* your agency, so selecting its members is of the utmost importance. They will represent you and help you attain your goals of professionalism and dignity. How they dress, talk, and conduct themselves sets the tone of your office. Choose personnel who will further the image you want at all times. Above all, your employees must be able to relate well to people—they must really *care* about your clients.

The ideal travel agent is well educated, well traveled, and well mannered. This combination, I admit, is hard to find, and an applicant with those qualifications is snapped up immediately. But try to choose someone with potential. Over the years you will invest quite heavily in employees in salaries, training courses, familiarization trips, and time. Be sure you have good material to start with.

You might find it difficult to hire just the right person, but you probably will not have to worry about a dearth of applicants. There will be times when you think that all the world wants to work in a travel agency. Agents receive many calls each week from would-be employees attracted by the lure of travel.

THE OFFICE MANAGER

We have already discussed the hiring of an office manager. He or she sets the example (along with you) to the rest of the staff in dress, conduct, and poise on the job. A manager must create harmony in the office, encouraging the other employees to work pleasantly together. A manager will settle any dispute between personnel, and on rare occasions (we hope) between the demanding client and the agent who is finding it impossible to fulfill those demands. The manager will always be loyal to a good employee who is doing his or her best, but must at the same time be fair and soothing to the client—no easy task.

The manager initiates sales promotions and acts as host at social evenings sponsored by the agency. When the public is invited to a film show where airline personnel are not present, the manager explains the film and answers questions. Managers are responsible for the sales report; reordering of ticket stock; interviewing potential commercial accounts; and talking to visiting representatives from airlines, steamship companies, and hotels. They will interview potential employees and usually have a free hand in hiring and firing the staff they supervise.

VALUABLE CHARACTERISTICS
OF THE STAFF

A new agency with quickly increasing business would do well to hire experienced help. If the owner has no previous travel experience and only the manager really knows the business, the manager will be very relieved to have a knowledgeable assistant. In an interview the office manager can assess the extent of an applicant's knowledge.

When hiring experienced help, though, be careful that the potential employee is not too specialized for your agency at its present stage. As agencies grow, especially if they have many commercial accounts, they usually divide the work into two distinct sections—commercial and vacation—rather than having everyone handle all the business. Agents are apt to prefer one or the other type of work, according to their temperament and abilities. But don't hire an expert in one field if you need an all-around agent, able to handle all clients. The vacation client wants advice, hotel descriptions, and answers to questions on the available activities—tennis, casinos, scuba diving and so on. But a secretary in business just calls with a list of flights and hotels, simply to get quick confirmations and the best rates. Some staff persons have a real flair for the vacation business. Others will be oriented toward the corporate accounts. But you are wise to postpone specialization until your agency has grown large enough to afford it.

Ability to speak a foreign language is a plus—it is not a necessity—for a travel agent. If there are foreign-language-speaking groups in the agency's neighborhood, you would do well to have at least one agent who can cope with the languages involved. In an area with immigrants who have trouble speaking English, you would be surprised how quickly you can become an agent to the entire group if in your agency they can explain their travel problems in their own language. Have you ever tried to book a flight and find out times or costs in a language you do not understand? Because of one French-speaking employee, an agency I know built up a huge business with the local Haitian population.

For every travel agency employee, an ongoing interest in geography is a basic necessity. Prod your new agents to study an atlas. First, do they know the geography of our own country? Do they know the principal towns of each Carribean island and Mexico? Can your agents point them out on a map? What if a client wants to fly from New York City to Hamburg? There is no direct flight at present. If agents have no idea of the geography of Europe, how can they route the client?

TRAINING IS ESSENTIAL

Hire new employees one at a time so that each one can become absorbed into the office before it is necessary to hire someone else. The office manager can keep an eye on any new employee, experienced or inexperienced, to see that he or she is fitting in with the other members of the staff and the office routine. When you hire inexperienced help keep in mind that you will have to train this employee to become a knowledgeable agent. Some applicants might have studied the travel business in an evening course. That can be a definite help. If they have at least some basic knowledge, it will save you time and frustration. It is not easy to train a new agent and run a busy office at the same time.

After working for a few weeks a new agent should be sent to a basic training course. Such courses are invaluable. They give the new agent an understanding of the behind-the-scenes operation of an airline, which is helpful in any travel job. Even long-time employees can benefit from an occasional refresher course, especially since ticketing rules change so frequently. There is no substitute for knowing one's business. A good employee is worth training well, first in basic courses, later in advanced material. At the completion of the course agents have more confidence in their efficiency. They are stimulated in their work and are accurate in its execution. Well-trained agents who enjoy being ever more proficient in their field have a goal to reach for.

The Institute of Certified Travel Agents awards the title of Certified Travel Counselor (CTC) to agents who complete a five-section academic program in travel agency management concepts. Business experience and personal integrity are also requirements. Classes are held in many locations throughout the country for agents wishing to participate in this program, the cost of which is $425. You can write to:

The Institute of Certified Travel Agents
148 Linden Street
Post Office Box 56
Wellesley, Massachusetts 02181

The lack of actual standards of proficiency has long been a problem for the devoted travel agent. But now growing professionalism in the field is apparent in the number of travel courses being offered in universities and adult education centers.

You have a right to expect your employees to work hard; but be understanding—you're probably learning along with them. Casualness and carelessness, however, have no place in a travel agency. The work is detailed and demands accuracy. If a ticket has not been properly validated, a passenger could be kept off a flight. You can imagine the repercussions of that mistake.

Employees who tend to be argumentative should be watched. Warn them that this behavior is not acceptable, and if they do not improve, let them go before they argue with a client. The clients' needs are of prime importance in any agency.

Watch out for the complainer. In any agency there will be some legitimate reason for complaints by an employee now and then. But chronic complainers are great destroyers of morale in any office. They are thus a danger to the loyalty of their fellow employees, perhaps causing office-wide dissatisfaction.

If an employee has a just grievance, discuss the problem and offer to solve it. If the employee stays on and continues to complain, fire that person without further hesitation. When he or she has left, call a meeting of your staff and find out if any dissatisfaction lurks anywhere. If anyone has a point to make, listen and consider it fairly. Be sure that harmony has been restored and that no atmosphere of animosity remains.

In addition to full-time employees, you will eventually have part-time help. The same rules govern both. Part-time workers must learn the job as thoroughly as other employees. Make sure they fill out files fully and accurately, so that when they are out of the office someone else can give all the facts to clients.

THE OUTSIDE SALES AGENT

In travel there is one more category of help: the outside sales agent. These agents are not salaried employees.

They are persons with access to large numbers of people who travel, groups or individuals, who book travel through them. These outside agents will book their clients in your agency, using your agency facilities, telephone, stationery, tickets, and so on. They are paid by splitting the commission in whatever ratio has been agreed on.

There are two types of outside sales personnel. First, there are the agents who come into the office on specific days and take care of all their bookings, mail, and messages. They do all the work on their clients' reservations and usually receive 50 percent of the total commission.

Second, there are the agents who do not do the work for the clients they refer to the agency. Frequently these agents work for a corporation and do not have time free for agency work. They are likely to have large numbers of referrals but their commission is lower than that of the agents who do the work themselves, usually 25 to 40 percent. These agents do not handle your office clients and they are not paid commissions on any customer who is already an office client. They deal with their own clients only, bringing you business that you would not have had without them.

A suggestion: do not take two outside sales agents who live near each other. They will know the same people, and there may be conflict between them about who can claim a particular client. Try to get outside sales agents from different areas, so that they cover a wider range.

Each employee in the agency must be willing to go to great lengths to keep clients happy. The entire staff, including part-time and outside sales agents, must be accommodating and caring and make clients feel that their wishes will be turned into fact.

11

Your Clients— How To Handle Them

Clients are the backbone of the business; if you have no clients you can forget all the rules and advice—you have no business. So you not only have to attract clients into your office but also keep them there as repeat customers.

Clients come in endless varieties—the pleasant, the irritating, the cooperative, the argumentative. For the agency, however, it is more meaningful to divide them in a different manner. There is the casual inquirer on the telephone, the stranger who drops in for an airline ticket, the vacationer who makes visits to decide on a two-week holiday, and the business person who is regularly in touch with constant travel needs. Your job is to make them all think of you as their regular travel agent. You want to be listed in their personal telephone book along with their doctor, lawyer, and dentist. You want to claim them as "your" clients.

In the last chapter we established that the staff *is* the agency. Add to that the fact that the client *is* the business. What emerges is the fundamental factor in running a travel agency—the relationship between the staff and the clients. The procedures of establishing and conducting an agency are strictly guided by conference rules; even furnishing the office is largely dictated by the necessities of paperwork, telephones, and other commercial needs. Now you are on your own, and it is right here, in this vital area, that you have your chance to make your agency better than any other—to add your own ideas and extra touches, to raise your performance above just good service and careful work. *The relationship between the staff and the clients cannot be stressed enough.*

What is the agent's real duty to the client, aside from the obvious jobs and services? There are three main areas that I consider essential—and though they seem obvious, it is easy to make mistakes on these important points.

WHAT DOES THE CLIENT WANT?

When your client comes into the office for a ticket from Chicago to Las Vegas obviously there is no question about how to handle the matter. But figures established by a survey of travel agencies show that each year more and more clients rely on their agents to assist them with a choice of destination. If the clients know they want to ski, it's an easy task for the agent to compare the merits of Aspen, Colorado, and the Laurentians, Quebec. But some clients are even undecided about the type of vacation they want. Toss out a few likely ideas—sightseeing, golf, fishing—and each time watch for a reaction. If there is none, try more out-of-the-ordinary suggestions—

barge trips, music festivals, architectural tours. Originality is often the cure for indecision or boredom.

Listen attentively as your clients tell you what they have in mind for a vacation. If they are new clients you should be watching for clues to what they enjoy—swinging nightlife, sports, casinos. Do they care about good food? Will they want luxurious accommodations or just an average room in which to leave their possessions while they rush off to sightsee? You can find the answers to these questions not only by asking directly but also by listening to what they tell you about past vacations. I've known many clients who said they would like a nice, small, quiet hotel and then proceeded to tell me about the marvelous casino they enjoyed nightly in the Bahamas "right in the hotel . . . really great . . . five different restaurants right there in the lobby!" Don't take these swingers at their word and send them to "Recluses' Retreat!" Sometimes clients say one thing and mean another. Learn to listen. When clients say one thing then give signals that they mean something different, keep on listening until you know what they are really after.

WHEN YOU KNOW WHAT THE CLIENT WANTS— GIVE IT TO HIM

Sounds simple. What tends to undo conscientious travel agents in this matter is the emphasis put on giving service and their earnest desire to do just that. The client tells you where he wants to go and says, he is interested in the Rainbow Hotel. You have seen the Rainbow Hotel and have put it on your "don't use" list: it's noisy, its clientele is at the opposite end of the spectrum from either Emily Post or the social register, and service is to be had only at the bar. You gloss over the Rainbow Hotel and extoll the virtues of the lovely little inn where the furnishings are beautiful and the food and service are just right. Why haven't you seen that client again? Because he is probably in the Rainbow Hotel, courtesy of another travel agent. Your job is to let the client know what type of hotel he is considering, in case he has been misinformed, but without putting it in a negative light and therefore implying that his taste is poor. He will then let you know if that is what he wants. Remember, the hotel you think of so fondly might be utterly wrong for your client, but the one you couldn't wait to get out of may be his idea of paradise. The ability to gauge what other people want is an important part of your job. Assess the client's character, his likes and dislikes, and listen to what he tells you.

When discussing an airline reservation tell the clients which carriers service the route and ask if they have any preference. If they have, honor it, even if they are not insistent about it. Businesspeople traveling internationally frequently prefer an American carrier in order to support the American economy rather than that of a foreign country.

I once defied my own rule in this matter. I had as a client the executive of a large business corporation, who traveled to Europe twice a month and did not enjoy traveling. As a client he was pleasant and cooperative, yet he was tempermental and particular about comfort. As you can imagine, I made every effort to make his journeys as easy and pleasant as possible. He liked the 10:00 A.M. flight from New York so that he could arrive in London in the evening to get a night's sleep before meeting his business associates the next morning. One day I became especially helpful and suggested that as a change from the American carrier he habitually flew, he might, just for once, enjoy the services of a foreign carrier. He agreed, and all arrangements were made.

On the morning of his departure, I had just entered the office when the telephone rang. There was Mr. Executive, almost jumping through the telephone in rage. He had been bumped. He was told that some mistake had been made and his reservation was for economy class, and that the airline would be glad to offer him a seat there—which he refused in no uncertain terms. Mr. Executive told me very clearly what he thought of my suggested airline and informed me that he would not move from the bar at Kennedy Airport until I straightened everything out. With the flight heading for the runway at that very moment, I knew that this was a lost cause. I called the reservation department of the airline involved, and as I had expected, was told that their records showed that my client's reservation was for economy class. I had personally booked this reservation in first class and rechecked it myself several times. My client ended up leaving on the evening flight—angry, tired, and more than a little worse for the wear!

I do not recount this story to be detrimental to the carrier concerned, which happens to be among the finest. Nor do I tell it to suggest superior service by American carriers. The incident described, including denial of guilt, could just as easily have happened with any airline. My representative for the U.S. carrier which my client habitually flew happened to visit my office in the midst of this commotion. When I told him what was going on, he laughed and said, "It happens on any airline. You know it and I know it, but you will never make the passenger believe it." His remark is the whole point of the story. Had the client selected the carrier, he would have been angry—but only with the airline, not with me. In this instance, the responsibility was entirely mine. Fortunately, by the time he returned, he had simmered down a little and merely greeted me with "Never put me on a foreign carrier again"!

No airline exists on which some passenger has not had a bad experience and never wishes to use it again. But such experiences do not reflect negatively on the overall reputation of one carrier nor of the airline industry as a whole. Again, the point to be learned is this: listen to your clients and honor their preferences.

STRAIGHTENING OUT CLIENTS' MISCONCEPTIONS

"Seven days—Rio de Janiero—$200!" suggests to most clients that they can fly from their hometown (where they are reading the advertisement in the newspaper) to Rio and stay there in a hotel for seven days and fly home again for the total cost of $200. A telephone call to the source of this advertisement is likely to uncover the facts—that the $200 represents only hotel costs (per person, in a double room) and that airfare is not included. You cannot fulfill the hopes raised by these misleading advertisements, but you can at least find out the correct information and suggest to your client the best alternative package that you know is a legitimate good value.

Clients cannot be expected to know the rules existing between airlines and agents, and at times they expect favors which the agent is unable to grant. Although polite service is your motto, there are times when you must be firm. The client's misconception of your authority must not push you beyond ethical behavior. Such a situation arose with a regular, difficult, and somewhat flamboyant client of mine. She was European, with an inclination to fly to various cities in Europe at very short notice. On this occasion she had impulsively decided to go to Rome, accompanied by her current boyfriend. I issued the tickets and wished them well.

The following day, her boyfriend appeared in my office demanding a new set of tickets. I told him that this was impossible, and asked him what happened to the ones I had given him. He matter-of-factly explained that he and my client had a fight the previous evening and at one dramatic moment the angry woman had ripped the tickets into a thousand pieces and danced on them. He could see no reason why I couldn't simply rewrite the tickets—the woman, after all, was a good client.

I explained that I would be required to pay the airlines for the tickets I had issued and that I could issue new ones only on repayment, for I would have to pay for these also. He flew into a rage, and some time passed before he was calm enough to be told, both by me and by the airline on the telephone, that his only solution was to purchase another set of tickets and I would submit a lost ticket claim for the destroyed ones. Provided no one used the tickets for a flight (unlikely considering their condition), they would receive a refund after the expiration date of the validity of the tickets—one year. (All tickets, except those at discount fares, have a validity of one year.)

In handling clients be tactful but firm; make it clear that you know your business and will conduct it in an ethical manner. Help them find out what they want and give them all the advice they need for their vacation or business trips, and they will remain your clients for a long, long time.

12

Selling The Vacation Market

PACKAGE TOURS

The simplest and most common type of vacation travel sold today is the package tour put together by tour operators or wholesalers (American Express, Maupintour, Globus, and many others). They come in two main types: independent and escorted.

Independent Tours

These tours normally include airfare, hotel accommodations, transfer service between airport and hotels, and one or two sightseeing trips. The clients, being provided with these essentials, are free to spend the rest of the time as they wish.

Escorted Tours

These tours provide air transportation, hotels, and transfers, and also continue to take care of the passengers throughout their stay. In the daytime there is sightseeing or perhaps coach transportation from one city to another, and meals are frequently included. Because the members of such tours spend most of their travel time together they often form friendships. Also, they see and learn much more than they would be likely to on their own, especially on a first visit to a country or region. Good tour escorts are like friends who are natives of the area. They know history as well as geography; they know the local architecture; they know the best shops and restaurants; and they can solve any problems that might arise in hotels. They always speak several languages and have outgoing personalities. And if they are doing their job at all well, everyone falls a little bit in love with them.

Good advice can also be found in a guidebook. But because tour escorts have led this same tour several times recently, their advice about which restaurants have now become tourist traps and which shops have raised their prices is absolutely reliable.

On both types of tours the prices given apply to standard hotels. Should the client want upgraded accommodation, the brochure lists appropriate hotels and prices, other elements of the tour remaining the same. Before booking these tours, draw your client's attention to the tour conditions on the back of the brochure, particularly the cancellation penalties. Remember to have your client sign the disclaimer waiver, which we have already discussed (page 98).

When the client chooses a tour, make the reservation and send a deposit to the wholesaler immediately.

Final payment is normally due six weeks before departure. The wholesaler then mails the documents to you (certificate of participation in the tour, hotel confirmation, itinerary, and airline tickets if these are to be issued by the tour operator). Where permissible write the airline tickets in the agency instead of getting them from the tour operator. This helps to increase your volume of airline sales.

INDIVIDUALIZED TRAVEL

There are always clients who want totally personalized travel. For them the agent works out an individual itinerary, choosing cities, hotels, sightseeing tours, and transfer service at each stop. In the trade these individual inclusive foreign itineraries are referred to as FIT (foreign independent travel).

In the first interview with FIT clients, you should establish exactly which countries and cities they want to include. Start by selecting the flights. Keep in mind that a day when a traveler changes locations is almost a day lost. By the time one checks in at the airport an hour before departure, completes the flight, goes through customs upon arrival, and drives to the new hotel, even if the flight was not a long one, most of the day is gone. Avoid arranging extremely early morning flights; after all, the passenger is on holiday. Try for a departure around 10:00 or 11:00 A.M. throughout the itinerary. In this way the traveler can reach the destination, get settled in the new hotel, and still have part of the day to explore new surroundings.

You have still other considerations. For example, does your client qualify for an excursion fare? If so, how many stopovers are allowed? If your client is not going to fly within Europe, are you responsible for drawing up a driving itinerary day by day? Are you going to work out a detailed itinerary using rail transportation? Will you choose sightseeing tours? It is wise to avoid sightseeing tours on the day of arrival or departure. Delays can occur, and anxiety should not be your client's lot on vacation.

When the object of a client's tour is to visit religious shrines, find out if there is a day of the month of special interest at that particular spot. The sixteenth of each month is a day of pilgrimage to Fatima in Portugal, for example. When visiting Lourdes or Fatima on special days, allow plenty of time, since traffic will be extremely heavy in the vicinity of the shrine.

When you have the itinerary worked out on paper and have your client's blessings to go ahead with it, obtain a sizable deposit. Next call a wholesaler and request your selected hotels and sightseeing tours; transfers too, if they are included. Ask the wholesaler for a price on the services he or she is supplying. It will take about two or three weeks to get confirmation on this list of requests. If a chosen hotel is unavailable, you must now select a substitute. (Alternately, you can book the hotels directly through their reservation system.) Upon confirmation of the land portion, the wholesaler will request a deposit, and final payment should be made six weeks before departure. It is reasonable for the agent to add a service charge per city for the work done on an FIT.

Not all agents are sufficiently knowledgeable to handle FITs; it is one of the tests of a good, experienced agent. To do a good job takes personal knowledge of the area involved and an ability to assess a client well.

The advantage to the clients of an individual itinerary of this type is that they are totally independent, even in the choice of flights. They can distribute their time as they wish, staying in any city as long as they want. They can use hotels that do not cater to groups—small, somewhat inexpensive, well-run hotels they would not find on group accommodation. When FIT clients have confidence in their agent, they will return regularly.

Today, FIT clients are the exception rather than the rule, but the wealthier the clientele, the more FIT work an agency will do. It is luxury business and demands exceptional service. For example, I include a list of restaurants, shops, and art galleries which I think the client will enjoy in each city.

What if you are required to plan an FIT in an area you do not know well? First, read about the area in a travel guide. Then call the representative of the country's airline, such as South African Airways, for advice on that country. Ask him or her for help with the itinerary. This will be especially helpful if the representative is a native of the country of destination, which is often the case.

Never ignore advice and decide to bluff through—in that way lies disaster. I know one agency owner who refused to believe that real knowledge of the country was the first essential in approaching an FIT. He had clients who were going to make a long tour of South America and wanted to drive part of the way. This agent, in ignorance, routed them over the Andes by car. The situation was saved by a horrified employee who read the file, rushed to the phone, and sent an SOS to the airline representative. Never be afraid to say you are personally unfamiliar with a particular area. You can't have been absolutely everywhere. Simply obtain the information from a reliable source. This is similar to the medical situation in which a general practitioner calls in a specialist.

ESCORTING A TOUR GROUP

You have a twofold reason for accompanying a group on a tour: (1) to ensure the smooth functioning of all services contracted for and (2) to promote good feeling among the tour members and make the occasion so enjoyable for all that you will get repeat business.

When you have been an agent for several years, you will find that without realizing it, you have had an almost professional education as a tour escort. Agents' familiarization trips are almost always escorted, and you can learn the routine from repeated observation of the escorts.

Anyone who has ever been on an escorted tour is aware of the escort's duties: looking after the passengers and baggage, checking in and out of the hotels, solving all hotel problems, posting times of tours and meals on hotel notice boards, checking in at airports, and assigning seats for smoking or nonsmoking preferences. As an agent in charge of your own clients you must combine the responsibilities of the professional tour escort with those of a host entertaining important guests.

To accomplish all this, you must be well organized, and to be well organized, *you must make lists*.

To start with, make numerous copies of the passenger list. You may want to hand one out to all members of the group to help them identify their traveling companions. You definitely will need many copies for yourself. Use one copy to list the number of pieces of luggage checked through by each person. Use another to list each member's hotel room number in each city so that you can contact that person immediately if necessary. And use one copy to check off who is going on any optional tour. Also make flight lists and hotel lists, and bring all your letters of confirmation with you.

Even if the tour group has special luggage tags, it is a good idea for the tour conductor to buy yards of a brightly colored ribbon (such as electric blue or bright green). Give each passenger a piece of this ribbon to tie on each piece of baggage being checked through. That ribbon helps to identify your group luggage quickly when it comes off the baggage turntable. The less time you have to linger at an airport, the happier your group will be.

You must not lose passengers, and you must not lose baggage. Never make a move without counting both, particularly when checking in and out of airports and hotels. On sightseeing tours, no matter how many stops are made, count the passengers before leaving. (Some may well deserve to be abandoned, but resist the temptation.)

Most tour conductors collect the passenger tickets and passports rather than merely keeping a list of those numbers. If a passenger were to lose a passport, you'd have a hard time trying to look out for both the group and the unfortunate passenger. Take charge of these vital documents, so that the tour is not disrupted.

Most cities throughout the world require local tour guides to be hired for city sightseeing. Welcome this rule; you could not offer either the knowledge or the local flavor of the local resident. On these occasions become one of the group and enjoy it, or use the time for relaxation if the tour is a long one. Be sure to do your homework before you leave, even if local tour guides are used, so that you can discuss intelligently what you are seeing and be at least as well informed as your clients.

Your Role as Host

If meals are included and the group is going to dine together, unlike the professional tour escort who is entitled to privacy at meal times, you must now play "host," joining the group and keeping up a party spirit. If meals are not included and the tour members break up into small groups (we hope not cliques) for dinner, you have a rather more difficult path. You must not habitually become part of any one group. There are two ways to avoid the problem: (1) tell the entire group that you are going to the corner "trattoria" and can recommend it to anyone who is interested; (2) make restaurant recommendations to the group but state that you have business to take care of and will not be free to join them.

If daytimes are spent on tour, join a different group each day for lunch—of course making sure no one is left out. You must help the group members get along well together and enjoy your company at the same time. At each hotel remind the tour members to check the bulletin board for information concerning the group. List your room number so that you can be reached if anyone has a problem.

You'll be exhausted by the time you get home, but if you've done the job well, you'll have a very good chance of booking the same group on its next trip.

FOREIGN CLIENTS

No matter where your agency is located, you will meet people from all parts of the world: a scientist from India who has come to study, U.N. diplomats, a Latin American seeking a better-paying job, a German housewife visiting her daughter, a Japanese businessman from Tokyo—they may all be your clients, even if only for a brief time. Do not offend them by ignorance of their countries or their customs. Even the mention of home can be uplifting to many expatriots. I once had a tall, strong but dejected man walk into my office and say, "I want to go back to Honduras." I said, "You want to fly into San Pedro Sula?" The dejection vanished. He lit up and said, "You know it?" I told him that I had never been there, but he remained overjoyed that I knew something about his country.

As an agent you have become part of the international world. You will travel a great deal, and in your office you will be host to all nationalities. You're a representative of your country as well as your own office. In this rushed, impersonal world everyone treasures a place where they are received warmly and where their wishes are catered to.

We have all heard the cliché that travel is broadening. But this is true only if you leave your preconceptions at home. As a habitual traveler you will have learned not to use your own country's lifestyle as a standard for other cultures. The sophisticated, intelligent, young man from Bombay, who is a graduate from Oxford university and tells you entertaining stories of his carefree bachelor days there, explains to you very seriously that his marriage was, of course, arranged by his parents, and why this is the sensible approach to marriage. You do not have to agree, but you should suspend your judgment until you have considered the point of view of a totally different culture. Then, whether you are in a foreign country or overseas visitors are in yours, you will have discovered the greatest joy travel has to offer.

CRUISES

Now let's consider clients who want to go on a cruise. Find out the approximate date they would like to leave and how long a cruise they have in mind. Are they thinking of the Caribbean, the Mediterranean, or any other specific area? Check in the *Official Steamship Guide* for the selection of sailings. Use all your knowledge to help your passengers make a happy choice. Find out from the cruise line the availability on the cruise selected. Find out the cost of the cabins available: the higher the deck and the more central the cabin, the higher the price. Price is also determined by the size of the cabin and the type of facilities included. ("Facilities" refers to bathroom.) Do your clients want an inside or outside cabin? Outside cabins have portholes; inside cabins do not and consequently cost less.

The shipping reservation clerk can tell you the price range and the types of cabins available. If the cabin and price sound right for your client, you can ask to take an option on the cabin. This means that the shipping line will hold this particular cabin for your clients for about a week. By the option date, you must send a deposit representing a quarter of the total cost to the shipping company to reserve the cabin. Full payment is required six weeks before sailing.

Get out the deck plan of the ship when the line offers a cabin to your client. Point it out to the client and be specific about describing it. If it has an upper and lower berth rather than two lower berths, say so. By studying the deck plan passengers will have a good idea of the location of their cabin in relation to the stairways, halls, restaurants, and so on.

Cruise passengers vary from those desiring the ultimate in luxury to those barely able to afford the lowest-priced berth. To the affluent client you offer deluxe accommodation, stressing service. To the economy-minded you point out that even if the least expensive cabin is next to the engine room, they won't be spending much time there anyhow. Their days will revolve around the deck, swimming pools, lounges, and other public rooms. Tell your clients the time for meals at first sitting and second sitting on the ship they have chosen, and ask them which sitting they prefer. Offer to book their dining room table for them.

Sell your cruise clients the shore excursions. You'll pick up the commission and save them from standing in line in the ship's lounge to purchase these tickets from the tour operators.

Selling the cruise market pays. Cruises give clients excellent value, whether they purchase minimum or deluxe accommodation. It is a total vacation; everything—rooms, meals, entertainment—is contained in the price, and you get commission on the total package. Here are some interesting facts to consider:

- Travel agents sell 98 percent of all cruise business.
- Only 3 percent of the population has been on a cruise; you can expand this market right up through the remaining 97 percent.
- Cruise passengers are often repeat customers—in fact, they frequently make the cruise an annual event.

There is an enormous variety in cruise ships and their itineraries. Get to know what each line is offering so that you can give your clients good advice and a full spectrum of choice in itineraries and accommodations. The sales representatives can supply whatever information you need. For repeat clients, try to select an itinerary that offers ports of call they have not previously visited.

First-time cruise passengers will always want information on the type of clothing to bring. Do warn clients that certain ways of dressing are inappropriate. Women, even very young women, should not wear short shorts in Caribbean towns, despite the climate. The native women are conservative in dress, and tourists should not, even innocently, give offense. Women should wear a head covering (scarf or hat) before entering a cathedral. Remind your clients of this requirement so that they will not be disappointed by being refused admission.

Remind all clients going to hot climates to bring and use suntan lotion and clothing to cover the head and arms. Clients should be sure to bring with them any medication they require. It is very frustrating to try to fill a prescription in a foreign country. In certain areas (Mexico and Brazil) a warning about drinking the water is in order—better stick to the bottled variety.

It is a custom of most travel agencies to send to the ship a bottle of champagne for cruise passengers. I send a signed bon voyage card with a check to the catering department and request that a bottle of champagne and the card be presented to my client at dinner the second night out. This festive touch adds to the gaiety and luxury which a ship epitomizes.

REQUIRED DOCUMENTS

Any time passengers make an international journey it is your responsibility as their travel agent to inform them about the documentation required. It is customary for travel agents to keep passport application forms in the office, as a service to clients. Citizens of the United States fill out these forms, include two photographs and a check for thirty-five dollars, and bring or send these papers to the nearest courthouse. They should allow at least three weeks for a passport to be issued. An American passport is valid for ten years from the date of issue. For those under eighteen, passports cost twenty dollars and are valid for five years.

A husband and wife, sisters, brothers, or an entire family can use one passport among them if they so desire. I always recommend that each individual have his or her own passport. No one can enter a foreign country without a passport, and if one member is called home hurriedly, complications could arise on a joint passport.

A *passport* is issued to citizens by the government of their country. It officially establishes their identity and nationality, permits them to travel to foreign countries, and assures their right to reenter their native land.

A *visa* is a permit to a national of one country to visit another. The visa is officially stamped into the subject's passport by the consul of the country to be visited.

Always be accurate regarding the requirements for the countries on a client's itinerary. If a visa is required your client will not be allowed to enter the country without one.

Advise your clients sufficiently ahead of time when inoculations are necessary. It's no fun to be greeted with a yellow fever shot the minute you set foot in a new country. Documentation is different for nationals of each country. Do not assume that your client is an American citizen—ask. There is no use giving the requirements for a U.S. citizen to a French citizen, even one who lives in this country.

When you make cruise reservations ask the shipping lines what documentation the passenger must bring. When only proof of U.S. citizenship is needed, a passport, even an out-of-date one, will do; voting registration or discharge paper from one of the U.S. armed services also suffices. A driver's license is not good enough. Resident aliens should carry their resident alien card and passport.

Impress on your passengers the need to look after this documentation carefully—especially passports. Any tour guide can tell you that this is not as automatic as you might think. If your clients get into trouble half a world away, who do you think will come to their minds as a likely source of help? Their consulate, you hope. But many clients don't think that way. Who always knows what to do? Their travel agent, of course. Just hope their phone calls are not collect.

13

The Commercial Account

When an agency handles all the travel needs of one particular firm or corporation, that arrangement is called a commercial account. These accounts are greatly to be desired. Businesspeople are constant travelers, regardless of season or economic ups and downs. They are a guarantee of year-round business. Several good commercial accounts help put a solid foundation under any agency.

When your agency is new and just starting to build up volume, do not immediately chase after huge corporations. You will not, at this early stage in your agency life, be able to handle their needs. Approach them later when you have the ability and the resources to service them well. Start by going after the smaller businesses.

Be aware that commerical bookings are more subject to change than vacation travel. These itineraries, therefore, are frequently redone several times over. For example, Executive A requests a flight from New York to Los

Angeles on Wednesday morning. His flight is booked, his ticket written and in his possession; then, on Tuesday afternoon, you get a call from his secretary. Executive A will not be able to leave tomorrow morning. Could you get him a flight on Thursday afternoon? And instead of returning directly to New York, he will now be going to Dallas on his way back. You now must cancel the first itinerary and start all over.

GETTING THE ACCOUNT

Make a list of small- to medium-sized businesses or corporations in your area, select the ones you consider good prospects for your agency, and find out the names of their vice presidents or other executives who have authority to designate their travel business. If you have a contact, use it. If not, write to the vice president of each company. In your letter, state your educational and professional background; mention whether you are a Certified Travel Counselor (CTC) and whether your agency is a member of ASTA and ARTA. Briefly describe your agency: volume, staff size, type of automation (if any), and the services you can provide. Follow up the letter with a phone call to secure an interview. This is your chance to win the account. If your agency isn't large enough to have separate staff for vacation and leisure travel, suggest that the firm's business could be handled exclusively by two specific employees. It is not a good idea to promise any one person: that person could be away on trips at various times or absent for illness. Companies like to become familiar with the people taking care of their business; in fact, they consider such people almost as fellow employees—an extension of their own office.

When you have become a large agency, fully automated, with a large staff, and able to offer sophisticated service, then it is time to pursue large corporations.

You will go through the same steps to land big corporations, but more formality will be required in your presentation. Try to find a social or business contact to make the important initial connection. An excellent introduction and recommendation would be that of an officer of one of the business firms you already handle. Otherwise, proceed with a letter, as you did in approaching the smaller companies. Find out as much as you can about the company you want to handle, its products and their uses, its locations around the world, and which companies are competitors.

When you get an interview, cover all the points listed previously: give an analysis of how much additional work your present commercial staff could carry and at what point you would have to hire additional employees. You, too, are entitled to ask questions. You will be taking on big expenses in order to service a large account—more staff, more computers, back-office automation. Furthermore, all those additions might make larger premises necessary. So find out exactly how large a volume of business you are discussing. You will already have a pretty good idea from your own research before the interview, but pin down all the relevant facts.

After the interview send a thank-you letter to the interviewer, inviting him or her to visit your office and meet your commercial staff. This could help close the deal.

Delivery of Tickets

Usually companies insist that the agency deliver tickets to their place of business, and you will no doubt be glad to agree. But do realize that tickets will often be required on short notice. Remember, too, the many frequent changes. You might just return to your office after delivering tickets when the call comes in to change them. In larger cities, messenger services are available for a few dollars a trip, but most companies, although uncomplainingly paying hundreds of dollars for first-class tickets, are strongly opposed to paying delivery fees. Commercial accounts, however, are so valuable that if necessary you should deliver the tickets. Treat each account individually; consider the distance of their premises from yours and the volume of business their accounts provide.

Form of Payment

Look into the company's payment record. The concern is not *whether* you will be paid, but *when*. You certainly don't want to borrow money at high interest rates to cover the interval of time between your payment to the airlines and the company's payment to you. If a weekly payment bill is not suitable for the corporation, suggest that all tickets be paid by credit card at the time of issue. This will usually solve the problem to the satisfaction of both parties. The Air Travel Card (ATC) (formerly Universal Air Travel Plan—UATP) is being used more and more frequently by corporations for all flight payments.

Business travelers today are likely to give you several different credit cards to cover their itinerary: Air Travel Card for flights; Amex, Visa, or Mastercard for hotels; and Avis or Hertz credit cards for car rentals. The universal credit cards (Visa, Mastercard, American Express) can be used in payment for almost all types of service.

In the normal arrangement between the agent and the frequent traveler who pays by credit card, the client authorizes the agent to sign the client's name on the charge form, with the agent's own initials beside the signature. Keep a file of the various credit card numbers of your constant travelers. This process eliminates any need for billing or waiting for payment.

Service your commercial accounts to the hilt. Learn as much as possible about the company's frequent travelers, such as their usual class of service—first, business section, or economy—and their seating preferences in the plane. Then prebook their seats. Also check on their personal preferences regarding hotels or airlines and any special dietary requirements.

TRAVEL EXTRAS FOR BUSINESSPEOPLE

Business travelers are so valuable today that both the airlines and hotel industry are going to great lengths to cultivate their business. As an agent it is simple for you to offer these inducements and to take advantage of special offerings. Do your homework. Offer all the comforts that are available.

Almost all airlines have special sections of the plane intended primarily for the business traveler. This section is referred to by several different names by the various airlines concerned—business class, executive class, frequent travelers class. Always suggest this service to your business travelers, of course, with the exception of the executive who travels first class. The service in this section of the plane is excellent and greatly appreciated by travelers who must attend meetings at their destination.

Many airlines at present are offering various "rewards" for frequent fliers. Get the brochures and where necessary the application forms for these privileges. These inducements are very popular with business travelers who earnestly apply themselves to win certain points for a free trip for themselves and sometimes for their spouses as well.

Hotels are striving to get their share of the business market by offering various types of corporate rates. The corporate rate has no one definition. It can be simply a lower rate than that charged to the public for a specific room, or sometimes a middle-range rate is offered for the highest-priced room available at the time of checking in. Each hotel has its own policy.

Hotels are also competing by trying to add to the business traveler's comfort through VIP clubs. Check with the Sheraton, Hyatt, Hilton, and Marriott chains. Separate sections of some hotels are put aside for business travelers with special check-ins. These extras are yours to offer. You can raise your reputation with business clients by being knowledgeable about them.

VACATION VERSUS CORPORATE BUSINESS

Year by year corporate travel accounts for a larger share of the agent's total sales volume. The Louis Harris study in *Travel Weekly* reveals that the volume of commercial accounts grew from 37 percent of total agency volume in 1976 to 44 percent in 1981. The percentage of business to personal travel is as follows:

Type of travel	Automated agency (percent)	Nonautomated agency (percent)
Business	48	29
Personal	43	61
Combined	11	10

Is one more desirable than the other? The answer is apt to be based more on the temperament and inclination of the individual agent than on the potential of either phase of the market. Here's a summary of the pros and cons of each field:

Commercial Travel

Pro

- Constant volume of business gives high volume of earnings.
- Fast completion of each action; clients know what they want.
- Potential source of much leisure business.

Con

- Frequent itinerary changes; repetition of work.
- High expense of doing business; more staff and equipment.
- Fast pace of work—high pressure.

Vacation travel

- Groups—large profits.
- Possibility of building up override commissions.
- More leisurely pace of work.
- Satisfaction of using one's knowledge of areas and services.
- Requires more research.
- More reliance on third parties (wholesaler); must be sure of reliability of suppliers.

At the beginning of your agency career you will gladly accept any client who adds to your sales volume. Later, you might decide to handle only vacation travel or commercial accounts, or like most small-to-middle-size agencies, a combination of both. It is unlikely that you will set up a definite percentage for the total volume of each type. The average agency handling both sides of the business has a good general-leisure clientele and individual businesspeople and a few commercial companies.

After this point your preference might point you in one direction exclusively. This is a decision you will make after studying your sales figures for each area, and perhaps most important, deciding which clients you are happier servicing.

14

Building Up The Business

Members of the public are there, ready to travel. How will you reach them with the message that they should travel through you?

First, be sure that you have taken the normal steps to make your agency known.

ADVERTISING AND PROMOTION

List your agency in the Yellow Pages. People do look there for sources.

Advertise in the local newspaper. Show some imagination here. If your newspaper has a travel section on Wednesdays, put an advertisement there for a few weeks. Then switch tactics. Instead of in the usual travel section, next time place your ad in the food section where the housewife will see it, in the sports section, or even in section one, along with the international news. Note which ad draws best.

Advertise on radio. Try a spot on your local radio station when you have a really good trip to suggest. If you have a good voice, ask the station to let you make your own recording. Your clients will enjoy hearing your voice. You will be amazed at how much you can say even in one thirty-second spot.

Then take these further steps to promote travel sales.

Talk to shipping and airline representatives. Ask if they will share the cost of an ad with you if you advertise one of their packages.

Put out a newsletter. Most agents agree that a newsletter sent to all clients and any other prospect is an excellent way to promote business. Make the letter personal. Tell your clients of trips you and members of your staff have taken to find ever better destinations and hotels. Describe spots about to become popular. Include humorous happenings. Mention any group trips that the agency is working on. Get this letter out every three or six months, according to your finances and type of clientele. Clients become familiar with these letters and have been known to call the agency when they fail to receive one.

Sponsor social evenings. These should not be frequent—but they should be very special. There should be a specific point to the evening, such as a film on South Africa to promote a group tour to the area. South African Airways would be glad to provide not only a film but also their representative, who will probably come along to expand on the film, answer questions, and generally socialize. Serve wine and cheese, coffee and cake, or whatever suits your clientele and your budget. Your staff should be present, but emphasize the social aspect of the evening. It is more pleasant to rent a suitable room in a hotel than to squeeze this event into your agency unless your premises are spacious.

Use your window display to full advantage. Airlines and shipping lines will provide endless material. Use your imagination. It's free advertising.

Now, having brought the public into your agency, are you merely issuing tickets—or are you *selling travel?*

SELL FULL TRAVEL SERVICES

Each client who enters your office for a simple airline ticket should automatically leave with travel insurance as well. Did your sales agent check for further requirements: hotel, car, sightseeing? Include every possibility. The clients will like it. They will feel they are being cared for and protected. Always ask how they are getting from home to the airport. Sell this service whenever you can. Corporate executives often rate limousine service—a very nice commission for you.

When selling a vacation package, include meals. If the clients prefer to be free to choose local restaurants, take the trouble to research the area's restaurants for them and make recommendations—no commission, but a big plus in clients' appreciation.

Another touch of attention: each time a client goes overseas, enclose a leaflet describing the electrical voltage and outlets. This will save your client great frustration. These leaflets are available from

Franzus Company
352 Park Avenue South
New York, New York 10010

SPECIALIZATION

Your agency is unique. You must decide in what direction to go—whether to expand all-around sales or to determine what you are good at and apply yourself mainly in that area.

After your agency has been in operation for about two years, check through your ledgers (described in Chapter 9) to get an accurate picture of the type of agency you have established. The recorded figures will show you which services you sell most heavily, where your sales are weak, and most important, whether business or leisure travel represents the larger share of your income.

Statistics in the previous chapter showed the constant increase in the business sector of the agency market. Are those figures true for your agency? If they are, and if you enjoy the corporate side of agency work, pursue it further. Write to more corporations (as shown in Chapter 13) and try to win their business. Concentrate your efforts on the corporate market.

Is leisure travel your strength and your interest? If so, are you going after the most lucrative side of this specialty?

PROMOTING GROUP TRAVEL

Anywhere that groups form and gather, potential for group travel also exists. Go to the group and introduce yourself. Write a proposal or give the group two different ideas, complete with costs, to choose from. Do not offer a large selection of alternatives, however, or your group will never come to an agreement. When it has decided on a trip, block off the number of seats required with the airline; call a wholesaler and secure hotel rooms; and add sightseeing, transfers, and so on. It is the same as individual bookings, but you can multiply your profits by the number of people in the group.

You can find groups everywhere. For example, think of an exercise class at the "Y." I'll bet that several enthusiasts there would seriously consider a trip to a well-known spa—La Costa in California or Palmaire in Pompano Beach, Florida. Or consider the local gardening club: How about England in the spring, for a tour of country houses and gardens?

Certainly don't overlook the vacation club of any business company.

Also, never underestimate high schools as a source of group business. The French Club could go to France or to Quebec; the Spanish Club, to Spain, Mexico, or Puerto Rico. Some high schools teach German, Italian, and even Russian. They also often have a ski club—good for the western United States, Canada, or Europe. A word of advice: allow the teachers to help you. They know their own students; they know who are troublemakers and who can be relied on to take charge. These young people will probably be housed three to each room to keep expenses down. Let the students and teachers work out the rooming list for you. Then just hope that the school does not have a flu epidemic when the group is due to leave!

SIDELINE SALES

Perhaps you could add a complete travel boutique. Under present regulations the agency's area could not also be used for other sales. It would require a separate room and entrance. How convenient for a cilent to be able to pick up all the little travel necessities at once—

foreign electrical outlet plugs, converters, dual control hairdryers, immersion heaters, and small travel alarm clocks. The notion items alone are a delight: tiny clothes-line and pegs to hang across a hotel shower rail, pillboxes in bright colors, folding scissors, key rings, purses with several compartments for various currencies, small sewing kits, folding rainwear, and all kinds of cosmetic cases. Travelers might be eager to buy all these things once they have their tickets. An attractive layout of travel merchandise would make them feel that their trip is almost underway, tangible proof that they are really en route. It is also an excellent additional source of income. (But do remember ATC's ruling: don't put these tempting items among your agency's desks.)

If you prefer to stock large items, you could even consider selling luggage. Again, keep it separate from the agency's sales area.

BRANCHING OUT

When you reach the goal you have set for yourself in volume of business, you may have a new thought: if one office is successful, "wouldn't two be twice as good"?

The answer depends on what you ultimately expect of a branch office and also on its location. If you simply want more volume and more income you would probably do better adding to your present office and operation.

In its physical aspects, opening a branch office is like buying a second home as a vacation retreat: it means duplication of all the necessities.

Has one particular spot been catching your eye as a good location? By now you have a very good idea of what is required to make an agency successful, and your instinct may well be correct. You might develop a good situation if the prospective location is far enough from your office to give you access to a promising clientele out of your present reach but still near enough so that your existing agency could keep a paternal eye on the new location and serve as a home office.

Are you trying to land a corporate account that is quite a distance from your office? If the distance appears to be a problem, either to the company or to you (from the point of view of ticket delivery), perhaps a branch office could solve the problem. You would, of course, expect to pick up new local business also. Because of the ATC rule of no more than 20 percent of an agency's business coming from one source, adding business besides the corporate account would be mandatory as well as desirable.

The branch office will need a permanent office manager. You cannot be in two places at once. Reread Chapter 5 on hiring a manager.

These examples of a branch office will allow increased sales by reaching a wider area. If you are very ambitious, this process can be duplicated in several physical directions through multiple branch offices.

The definition of a branch office by ATC is "an additional authorized agency location," and a standard ATC application form must be filled out to have the branch office accredited. The ownership and corporate structure must be identical to that of the home office, which is held fully responsible, legally and financially, for the actions of the branch office. The primary name of the branch must be the same as that of the home agency.

You might even find that a branch office is so favorably located that its income potential is better than that of the home office; or for some other reason you might decide that the branch should become the main office, and the present main office become the branch. To put the change into effect you would take these steps: obtain an amendment to your bond; write to ATC giving your name, address, and agency code number of your present home office and the same information for the branch. Request the redesignation and state the effective date. Attach the bond amendment.

In forming a branch office, you can if you wish purchase an existing agency. In order to conform to ATC requirements, follow the guidelines for buying an agency set out in Chapter 4.

15

Automation

You can be an excellent agent and do very well without automation. But as your business becomes bigger and bigger—more staff, more records to file, larger telephone bills—you will undoubtedly begin to consider it.

Discuss automation with your staff before you install a system. Be encouraging if any employees are fearful or reluctant. They are worrying about their ability to master this new technique. Explain that their work can become easier, faster, and more professional. *Travel Weekly's* 1981 Louis Harris survey showed that 68 percent of all agencies have an automated reservation system and that both the output per employee and the agency sales volume increased greatly after automating.

The screen unit is referred to as the CRT (Cathode ray tube). Lessons on how to operate it are given at the time of purchasing or hiring a computer. The keyboard is used to "bring up" information (flights, hotels, car rentals) on the screen and to print tickets and invoices. For the latter purpose it is connected with a printing machine normally placed in the agency's back office (printers are noisy).

Several major airlines have developed their own computer reservation systems (these are referred to as "hosted" by the airline). You can choose from several systems. When you decide to automate, talk to other agents who are using automated systems. Discuss the pros and cons of each system. Look for a system suitable to your volume and type of business.

The most frequently used systems at present are these:

- Sabre hosted by American Airlines.
- Apollo hosted by United Airlines.
- Pars hosted by TWA Airlines
- System 1 hosted by Eastern Airlines.
- Datas hosted by Delta Airlines.
- RESERVEC hosted by Air Canada (of interest to Canadian agents and marketed only in Canada).

Ideally computers used in travel agencies should show complete listings of all flights on a given route, time of flight departure, and availability of seats. They should in fact duplicate the complete choice of flights to an area as shown in the *Official Airline Guide,* but with the added advantage for the agent of seeing the availability of seats and fares in one quick glance. Without automation the agent must look up the destination in the OAG, select a suitable flight, call the airline (and probably be put on hold for some time), request the space, and give the client's particulars to the reservation agent. Further time is then spent in writing the ticket. The time saved by automation is significant—and obvious.

Automation, however, does not guarantee utopia. First, there is always the possibility of power failure or a malfunction of the machine. No matter how fully automated your agency becomes, continue your subscription to the *Official Airline Guides*, and also insist that all agents know how to write airline tickets. You will then be able to avoid complete immobility if the mechanical side of the business is disrupted.

At the present time, automated agencies also encounter another problem. Since the systems are hosted by individual carriers, they tend to be somewhat biased in their display of service and seating availability, the bias being, naturally, in the favor of the host. The carriers claim that this is not the case, but agents have found it to be so to such an extent that a few large agencies have invested in two different automated systems in order to detect bias and protect their own impartiality. The American Society of Travel Agents is directing its attention to this matter, and by the time you are ready to automate, the problem could well be solved.

In a busy office, one with a large corporate clientele, you need one CRT per agent. In a slower-paced agency, with mainly vacation travel, you could try one CRT shared by two agents. A small agency might even begin the automation process with one CRT and a ticket printer and increase the number of CRTs as the business volume picks up.

It would be impossible to list enough figures to show you what your cost would be. It depends on the number of CRTs and the number of printers you need. But here's a rough idea based on the SABRE system hosted by American Airlines:

Monthly costs for two CRTs and one printer: $500 including service. One-time installation charge: $600 ($300 is credited toward purchase if you decide to buy). Cost includes one-week basic training for two persons per CRT at American Airlines offices in Dallas, transportation included. Cost per ticket: 15¢; cost per invoice: 15¢; cost per itinerary: 15¢.

Small agencies considering automation but not quite ready to take the big step can hire a teleticketing machine without the CRT. This will give you the advantage of the professionally printed ticket, but you will continue to make your flight reservations by phone to the airline. The teleticketing machine is linked to the airline's printer at the airline's computer terminal. When you want the ticket you call the airline, go over the reservation that you made, and tell the airline to ticket. In a few minutes (if the airline is not backlogged) your ticket is printed out on the teleticketing machine in your office.

For information about teleticketing contact the two major suppliers:

RCA Service Company
Data Service Company, Building 204–2, Route 38
Cherry Hill, New Jersey 08358
Phone: (609) 338–4170
Cost: $117 per month; instructions given at time of purchase

Superior Teletypewriter Corporation
100 Louise Street
South Amboy, New Jersey 08879
Phone: (800) 631–8661
Cost: $128 per month; instruction on site at time of installation

As soon as agents have mastered the computer they begin to enjoy it. The swift access to fares and routing and the quickly printed ticket add up to more output per employee. The greatest benefit to the agency is the added ability to compete for and service the large commerical accounts.

After you decide on the automated reservation system best suited to your office, your next decision is whether to buy or rent. Discuss the costs for renting and buying with the sales representatives of the systems. Also bear in mind these other factors:

Purchase

- No monthly rental fee.
- Adds to agency's value.
- Can sell system—*but* it can become outdated.

Rental

- No large cash outlay.
- Service included in rental cost.
- Can change system when it becomes outdated.
- Option to buy is included in rental agreement.

Should you decide to rent, when you sign the lease be very specific about guarantees on repair service. How quickly will service be restored in event of a breakdown? You are talking in terms of hours or minutes—not days. If you buy your automation system, have a maintenance contract with a service company. (Ask the salesperson for information about service companies in your area when you buy the system.)

When your agency becomes really big you will probably consider further automation, computerizing your bookkeeping and accounting records. (This is referred to as "computerizing your back office".) It's a long way from opening your agency to computerizing your accounting, but be aware that this possibility exists. Perhaps an overload of work and phone bills drove you to automate your reservation and ticketing system. Pressure of corporate billing and record keeping could force you to do the same for the back office.

Back-office automation can be used to organize your records, speed up your billing and accounting process, and help you analyze your business. Your method of record keeping and your own business background are important in deciding what information you can obtain from your back-office system. Utilize the computer system to get maximum results from your expenditures. For example, you can check your advertising outlay against results. Your computer should be able to tell you what type of clientele you are drawing from each advertising source, which will help you isolate the clientele you want to reach for any given tour. The system can also be used for storing your ATC reports, keeping track of payroll expenses, and storing files.

If your agency has sizable corporate accounts to which you send bills for services, you will find automatic invoicing, statements, billing, and record keeping an absolute necessity. If you are interested in examining back-office automation systems, salespeople for any system will call at your office to discuss their product and your requirements. Always ask for names of other agencies using the system. Call these agencies and find out if they're satisfied. Also back-office computer systems are displayed at travel trade shows. Look around. Call American Airlines (SABRE system) and United Airlines (APOLLO system), who also offer back-office systems that tie in with their front-office machines.

The agent whose business is mainly commercial is apt to automate sooner than one whose clientele is mostly the vacation traveler. The business traveler has less choice and less room for personal preference than a client going on vacation. Business travelers take the flight most suitable for arriving in time for their meeting, and they stay at a hotel near either the business destination or the airport. The essense of this kind of booking is to book flights and hotels in the least time at the best possible price. An agent with several large commerical accounts certainly requires automation.

On the other hand, vacation travelers need advice about hotels, can choose among several flights, and might even want the agent's advice on which destination would best suit their holiday needs, pocketbook, and mood. That is where the agent's experience and knowledge count—experience in judging what the clients want and knowledge of the areas, hotels, and so on that can provide it. Only after such choices have been made will the agent go to the computer to check availability and exact prices.

Computers have made changes in many industries and certainly travel agencies have benefited by this development. As in other industries the computer heralds the wave of the future in travel.

16

Deregulation

Throughout this book many references have been made to the controlling bodies that govern the travel industry. Chapter 3 is devoted to a description of the responsibilities of each one. The overall purpose of these controls is to ensure safe, reliable, and ethical service to the public through the combined efforts of the airlines, travel agents, and other branches of the travel industry.

AIRLINE DEREGULATION

For forty years, 1938 to 1978, the airlines operated under the strict regulation of the Civil Aeronautics Board (CAB), which had the power to license carriers to service specific routes, approve or disapprove mergers between airlines, approve rates and fares, and assure that carriers did not engage in unfair or deceptive methods of selling air transportation to the public.

In 1975 Senator Edward Kennedy held hearings on the airline industry and concluded that CAB rules prevented competition in the field, to the advantage of the scheduled carriers. He suggested that CAB's authority should be lessened. At the same time, President Ford's administration became interested in deregulating the airlines. Debates and hearings continued until the Airline Deregulation Act was signed in October 1978 by President Carter.

This act gave the airlines greater freedom over routes and fares, and it also gave them freedom to choose the percentage of commission they would pay to travel agents. Before this time many agents had complained of low commissions and therefore, low incomes. They worried that after deregulation their incomes would decrease. The total opposite occured: all carriers raised their rates of commission. After deregulation the confusion of fares created hard work for agents, but it also brought more and more clients through the agents' doors as the confused public turned to the professional agents for advice. The result of these two factors, higher rates and greater confusion, was a huge increase in commissions. Agency commissions for the 17,000 agencies in the United States increased by $300 million in 1980 according to former CAB chairman, Alfred E. Kahn.

TRAVEL AGENCY DEREGULATION

By provision of ATC and the International Air Traffic Conference only the airlines or authorized travel agencies could sell airline tickets. But the ever-growing volume of this market did not escape Ticketron and other outlets. Ticketron requested the right to sell airline tickets, arguing that if more outlets sold tickets, prices would be lower. The fact that Ticketron wants to enter the travel market only proves how lucrative selling travel can be.

After deregulation of the airlines, CAB began a detailed study of competitive methods of distributing air transportation. In December 1982 the board made a decision to eliminate agents' exclusivity, making it theoretically possible for airlines to distribute their tickets through other outlets. At present the ruling applies only to tickets for domestic air service on one airline ("on-line" flights). Where two or more carriers are involved in any routing ("interline" flights) the ticket must be issued by the airline or an authorized agency. (These restrictions may be lifted in 1985.) An airline is not required to use new outlets for its tickets, but it may do so if it so desires.

The important question for travel agents is this: "How great a change will the CAB ruling make in their business?" The answer depends on (1) the airlines—how likely are they to use other outlets? and (2) the public—if other outlets exist, are people likely to use them in preference to travel agencies?

The Airlines

The travel agency is a highly efficient outlet for selling airline services. It is, in fact, less expensive for airlines to have their tickets sold by travel agencies than it is to open their own offices and hire and train their own personnel to sell directly to the public. Agents are the primary source of airline business, accounting for 65 percent of domestic and 85 percent of international ticket sales. Airlines have no intention of offending agents.

The ticket seller within the space of a week is in possession of a great deal of money belonging to the airlines. Agencies pass this money along through the regular channel of the agency sales report. Any less secure system would be unacceptable to the airlines, and to establish a similar system for individual outlets would be extremely difficult and costly. Let's hear the airlines' intentions, as expressed by their senior executives in an article in *Travel Weekly*, Dec. 20, 1982:

- "TWA has no intention of changing its already firm commitment to the agency distribution system as the primary purveyor of air travel to the public."—Brian Kennedy, vice president of advertising and sales, TWA

- Eastern intends to continue selling tickets "only through accredited travel agents or its own outlets."—Russell Ray, vice president of marketing, Eastern Airlines

- "We will do nothing differently."—John Zeeman, senior president of marketing, United Airlines

- "There are so many well-established, well-managed travel agencies providing service out there. That isn't going to change."—Robert L. Crandell, president, American Airlines

- "Travel agents are going to continue to be the major system of selling air transportation."—Randall Malin, senior vice president of marketing, US Air

The Public

Do not underestimate the intelligence of the public. Agents appointed under the present system officially represent the airlines. A ticket written by an authorized agent, using the agency identification plate and the airline plate, is honored worldwide. Why would the public take a chance? If anyone other than an appointed agent wrote tickets, there might be no guarantee whatsoever that they would be honored. What could the public expect of Ticketron, for example? Only the airline ticket. For advice, further knowledge, or information the client would have to rely on the qualified travel agent. The same situation already exists in other fields. It is now possible to deal in stocks with new types of brokers who merely buy and sell at the client's request; but when clients want advice, discussion, or service, they go to a regular broker.

There will certainly be some changes made. The present rulings are very strict, and some modification would present opportunities to agents to enlarge their outlook and increase their sales. But it is impossible to sell airline tickets with no control whatsoever. A control establishes who may own ticket stock and write tickets, and a control decides when and how payment for these tickets will be handed over from the seller to the carrier. This is the base for the existing system, and whatever experiments are tried, it will no doubt remain. At present the controlling agency is ATC. If ATC is disbanded in a few year's time, the Justice Department or the Department of Transportation will probably take over, and the result might be regulation very much like what we have today, but ideally, with more freedom to enlarge and develop our travel and travel-related sales.

The agents' best defense against any inroads that might be made on their business by outside ticket outlets is *professionalism*. You are the expert—your knowledge of the field is superior to that of any outsider. Keep widening your knowledge and improving your service. Today every industry faces the constant demands of readjustment to new competition; no business is without problems. Travel is no exception, but agents are in fact better off than ever before. It is a fortunate person who can open and build up an agency *now*. The field is becoming more professional and lucrative. Agencies have more chance than ever to grow, to use the advantages of automation, to keep abreast of the times, and to continue to increase their income.

17

Bigger And Better Profits

Let's assume you have now gone through the stages of starting your agency, becoming appointed, and learning the business. You have had the satisfaction of seeing your agency grow. You have no doubt traveled and enjoyed the benefits. You now face the next question— "How successful do you *want* to be?" The answer to this is not, automatically, "as big and successful as possible." The answer will vary with the type of agency you want to run and the type of life you want to lead.

There are many roads to success and many forms of success. Most agents relax at the point you have now reached. Certainly it is an enviable position. You have a good income, and all the travel you want is available to you. When you reach this point you have every reason to feel satisfied.

In Chapter 14 ("Building Up the Business") we discussed the wisdom of analyzing your present business before you decide to enlarge your operation or to specialize. If your ambitions reach further than your present level of achievement, it is time to examine your agency's business patterns again. Know exactly what you have before you take another step forward.

I have outlined five different roads to ever-larger travel profits. They are for the very ambitious, those for whom the striving is fun in itself. Most of them are new fields, and if you choose to move in one of these directions, you will add your own ideas of promoting your business to the heights of success.

Read through all five possibilities. Choose a direction from among them or not, as you wish. They are all tantalizing in the enormous scope they provide for success. They all demand hard work. But these fields are not overcrowded. They are wide open and offer unlimited possibilities.

1—INBOUND TRAVEL

Now that you have learned to send your clients on their way, I am going to present a totally opposite viewpoint. What happens to your clients after you have sent them, say, to Madrid? Someone else takes over and sees that they get to the hotel, takes them on sightseeing tours, and we hope, makes them feel welcome and protected throughout their stay.

Now let us think of all the European, Oriental, and other tourists pouring into the United States to spend their vacation—and their vacation dollars—here. They need those same services that Americans look for when they go abroad.

Services for inbound travelers is a whole new trend, a wide-open field with the possibility of making vast amounts of money. Think of 20 million overseas visitors spending $750 per person per year within the United States. (This was the figure projected by United States government statistics in 1980.) Currency fluctuations influence the inbound travel market to some degree, just as they influence the choice of destinations for Americans traveling overseas. When the Italian lira is very low in relation to the United States dollar, Americans will be drawn to Italy to take advantage of the bargains available to them in hotel accommodations, restaurants, and shopping. By the same reasoning, foreign travelers will flock to the United States when the dollar is low in relation to their currency. (If you handle both markets, the advantage to you is apparent—a downturn in one side of the business is offset by an upturn in the other.)

Think carefully before going into inbound travel. Certainly it is not for everyone. You can make your decision only after you know what is involved and what is required of you. First, both time and money have to be invested to set up this type of business. All travel work is detailed—the inbound field especially so—and when you have a large group to take care of, the hours can be long and trying. But it is fascinating if you like it, and there is plenty of money to be made.

Start with small groups, then medium, and tackle the large ones only when you are very sure that you can handle them. Inbound travel to your area from other areas of the United States and Canada is obviously an easier market than that from overseas, mainly because there is no language barrier.

When you send your own clients abroad, you are careful to select reliable suppliers. It is exactly this type of reliable, flawless arrangement you must now produce for your incoming groups. Check and recheck everything personally. Go to the hotel yourself, look at the rooms, talk to the manager, look over the dining room.

Has the group been given a well-placed table? Does the tour bus company have a schedule and are you positive it will be on time? Make sure the driver knows exactly the route to follow and how long to stop at each sightseeing spot. The group will complain if it is rushed through an interesting stop on the schedule.

When you start your inbound travel business you are likely to take charge of your first groups and act as tour guide yourself. But it will not be long before you realize that you must have a reliable number of tour guides to call on. A large part of the success of any tour rests with the guide. Foreign groups will need bilingual guides who may be found at nearby universitites. Expect to train them to take charge of your groups in the manner you demand. It is essential that they be responsible and reliable—your business reputation is in their hands.

Guides must know the area thoroughly. They should be prepared to discuss objectively with foreign tourists U.S. politics, education, and economic system. They may be asked questions about salaries in various jobs, taxation, and costs of food or services. The visitors are comparing their lives with yours; they want to know the basic facts of life in America.

Remember that your foreign groups will want Americana, so have one hotdog and hamburger lunch, a cookout if possible. What about a rodeo—what a hit that would be! If you can't provide a rodeo (if you are situated in downtown Los Angeles or Chicago, for example) you may be able to arrange a visit to a live television show. Look around your own area, and offer a mixture of town and countryside. For example, if you are in New England, take your group to a quaint small town for shopping and a clam chowder and fish lunch.

Perhaps you could find local families who would like to participate in a meet-the-people type of program as they do in Denmark, or even offer overnight family accomodations as they do in New Zealand on the sheep farms.

Does the incoming group have a special interest? Are they artists, plumbers, athletes? If so, arrange sightseeing at places of specific interest to them. You might engage a local celebrity or authority on their subject to address them.

The inbound travel field has the great advantage of allowing you to establish your own fees for the services you provide. In setting your fees with overseas companies, specify them in United States dollars. In pricing your services be sure to allow for unexpected expenses. You cannot control everything that happens, but you or your guides can react in a way that will reassure your groups if they have been inconvenienced through no fault of yours. For example, let me tell you an experience I had as a member of an incoming group in New Zealand.

Our flight from Christchurch to Invercargill (at the southernmost point of the country) was grounded because of bad weather. At short notice a bus was found for the considerable remaining distance. Unfortunately, the heating in the bus malfunctioned, and it was extremely cold. It was close to midnight when the bus with the all-but-frozen occupants pulled up outside the Hotel Te Anau (near Milford Sound). Then a beaming hotel manager leaped into the bus and said, "Hurry into the lounge, we have fires burning; drinks are on the house, and there's a hot buffet. We're sorry about the delay and the cold, but welcome." Obviously the tour escort phoned ahead to the hotel and was authorized to spend money. All was not only forgotten and forgiven but also a warm, happy impression was left with the tour participants.

If you decide that this field is for you, how will you

find your incoming groups? Remember that this is reverse business. Your clients cannot walk through the door. You must start from where you are and trace them back to where the business comes from.

For domestic groups call local branches of associations such as Rotary, Kiwanis, and Elks. The local branch frequently knows if other chapters of the organization intend to visit your area.

To find incoming groups from overseas, telephone and call on foreign tour companies that have offices in the United States. (Usually these are located in Los Angeles or New York City.)

For a lead to larger groups from overseas, contact

The Commerce Department
14th Street—between E and Constitution Avenues, N.W.
Washington, D.C.
Telephone: (202) 377–2000

This department assists international associations considering the United States as a site for meetings. It is anxious to promote travel to the United States and will be helpful to you in your request to provide services.

The American Society of Travel Agents has thirty-one overseas chapters. Get the addresses from ASTA in Washington and write to the areas that interest you for names of wholesalers. Send letters describing your qualifications and the services you are able to offer them.

List yourself in *Elkort's International Reception Guide*.

Check all tourist authorities and tourist boards of foreign countries in the United States. They know the groups in their countries which are considering trips here.

When you have some experience in handling inbound groups, join the Travel Industry Association of America, an organization for agents in this business. They hold meetings called Pow Wows, and they sponser an annual Pow Wow that is rather like a trade show. Participating parties hire booths and display their services. This is an excellent opportunity to make contacts, as hundreds of tour operators from all over the world attend. It is, of course, expensive to hire a booth and staff it, but in inbound travel you are dealing with bigger costs and bigger profits.

Do not expect your present agency staff to be able to handle this work as well as your normal business. Inbound travel will develop into a business itself, with a staff of its own, and that staff must be excellent. When you earn the reputation with wholesalers of being reliable, you will have a solid base from which your business can grow.

2—THE IN-PLANT AGENCY

Another new area has opened up to the travel agent—in-plant travel departments.

Until recently large corporations, such as IBM, General Motors, and U.S. Steel, had within their own business offices their own travel section staffed by their own employees for the sole purpose of handling their own business travel. This was called an in-plant travel office and was not open to travel agencies. Now, however, in-plant offices *can* be handled by travel agents.

The ATC defines an in-plant agency as "an additional authorized agency location on the client's premises." It does not have to be open to the public. If you agree to become an in-plant agency for a corporate client, you must file for authorization of the location with the conference.

The commission for in-plant business is at present 3 percent on domestic airline bookings. You will get the full percentage on international airline bookings, and of course, 10 percent on hotels, cars, and so on. The volume is, of course, large, otherwise the corporation would not require a separate travel department.

Let us examine the advantages of agency in-plant locations for each of the three entities concerned: the corporation, airline, and agent.

The Corporation

When corporations handled their own in-house travel division they were responsible for the salaries of their travel employees. The in-plant location when operating as an authorized branch of an agency, can be staffed by agency employees, company employees, or a mixture of both, and the salaries can be paid by either one. The agency usually pays its own employees and also a percentage of the corporation's employees working in the travel department. The corporation, therefore, saves on salaries and in addition gains the expertise of the professional travel agent conveniently at hand on its own premises.

The Airlines

A very substantial saving—7 percent—in the domestic market is realized by the airlines when an agency handles a company's business as an in-plant operation. If the company was a corporate account at the agency's own premises, the normal 10 percent commission would have to be paid instead of the 3 percent it receives as an in-plant agency.

The Agent

Any projected loss to the agent in accepting a lower commission on domestic air is offset by the volume of business involved. Full commission is paid on international airfares and on all other services. The large volume also insures the agency of override commissions where they exist, therefore raising its overall percentage of commission. Overhead is extremely low, usually confined to the agreed-on salary arrangement. There is no rent or decorating expense. Furniture and equipment are provided by the corporation. There is another huge advantage—in fact it is the reason that many agents become in-plant agencies—the opportunity to become known to thousands of employees who could become clients of the home agency for their leisure travel, both as individuals and as groups.

As a small, somewhat new agency considering in-plant operations for a firm whose business is mostly domestic, weigh the pros and cons carefully. Consider what percentage of the travel involves land arrangements. Decide if it would be to your advantage to handle the company as a commerical account from your agency.

An agent with a sound business education who has enjoyed and prospered in the commercial side of the travel business could find this field very lucrative. If this is your bent, study the subject carefully and decide if you will go after several companies with the object of making in-plant operations your specialty.

An outstanding example of success in the in-plant field is that of Brian Froelich of BPF Travel, Parsippany,

New Jersey, who within the space of four years, established ninety authorized in-plant locations, grossing over $220 million a year. Among his clients are the *New York Times*, NBC, AT&T, ITT, Warner Lambert, International Paper, and Philip Morris.

The In-plant Agency in Canada

The in-plant system has just been opened up for Canadian agents, and the rules (as given by Nadine Godwin in *Travel Weekly*, February 24, 1983) differ in some respects from United States in-plant systems.

- Canadian in-plant systems are called Travel Agency Corporate Account Appointments (TACAA).

- Only corporations purchasing one million dollars in air travel (domestic and international) annually will qualify.

- Applications for appointment for in-plant operations should *not* be made to Air Traffic Association of Canada. The in-plant sales agreement will be a three-way contract among the airline, corporation, and agent. United States airlines are expected to honor this agreement for use of their services.

- The commission is 5 percent on domestic air service (tickets for travel within Canada or between Canada and the United States). No part of this commission can be given by the agent to the corporation as payment to the corporation's employees.

- The agents, if they wish may take over the corporation's employees as part of the agency staff and pay their full salary.

- The agent can pay the corporation a "reasonable" rent.

- No international tickets will be ticketed at the in-plant agency. These are to be ticketed at the agency's own premises.

- The corporation will pay all tickets issued at the in-plant agency by using one specific credit card; any credit card may be chosen, but it must then be used for all sales.

- Air Canada will provide one reservation system CRT and one printer free to each in-plant location.

Since the field is new to agents in Canada, changes in the rules are to be expected. Contact the Alliance of Canadian Travel Associations (ACTA) for particulars.

3—INCENTIVE TRAVEL

Has an encyclopedia salesman ever called at your house and, after extolling the virtue of the item he is selling, proceeded to tell you that if he sells a certain amount he will win a trip to Bermuda? That is *incentive selling*— selling that offers a reward to a salesperson when a certain goal is reached. More and more frequently the reward is in the form of a trip. Moreover, this is not a competition with only one winner. Usually a goal is set that can be reached by many people—often a whole department—working together. The reward trip also usually includes spouses.

Think about it! If a hundred people achieve the incentive level, close to two hundred people (including spouses) will travel. Besides, this is usually an all-expenses included trip—meaning that air transportation, hotels, transfers, sightseeing, and all meals are included. Thus, incentive travel is a very lucrative field, and the great news is that it is also a rather new field with lots of room for more agencies to move in.

In medium-size companies incentive programs usually last from three months to a year. The longer the time covered by the program, the larger the award is likely to be. The program is run by the corporation's sales promotion manager, who with other executives of the company sets the target production level. You, the agent, have no part in setting the goal, but you have two important jobs: first, to ignite enthusiasm for the trip, and second to handle the trip so superbly that it will remain a highlight in the lives of the participants.

You will need to know what percentage of the projected increase in sales is to be set aside for the award and approximately how many winners and spouses are expected to qualify. Those figures give you the total allowance for the trip and the cost per person. This will be one of the deciding factors guiding your suggestions for the destination. If the company has conducted incentive trips previously, find out where they were. This gives you an idea of their preferences and avoids repetition. You will decide with the company production manager the time and place of the trip. Incentive trips are normally one week long.

As the agent in charge of the incentive program you have virtually become a member of the company for the duration of the program. You must be present at every meeting where the incentive program is discussed, beginning with its initial announcement. You are the important person at that event: you must be able to generate enormous enthusiasm for the destination, to make each employee determined that he or she is going to be on that trip. You must then keep the enthusiasm alive throughout the competition. You will get great support from the airline you choose as carrier. Airlines love incentive groups. They have special departments to deal with this type of travel, and they will supply you with endless and excellent materials to tantalize the contestants. The trip itself must be superb; it's not just another group tour. The passengers are *winners* and must be indulged and treated as VIPs.

This is the time to talk directly to the hotel manager where the winners will be staying; ask for VIP treatment and every courtesy the house can provide. Build into the cost of the trip at least one open-bar cocktail party, special sightseeing trips for the whole group, and a special event—a barbecue or beach party—depending on the setting. You must send one of your staff along to operate a full-time courtesy desk to fullfil every request and to see that the hotel carries out all its promises. Above all, keep the fun going. Every day must have its special surprises. This is not a quiet group looking for peace and quiet; the whole trip is one big party. Have a photographer present on sightseeing trips and at cocktail parties and post the pictures on the hotel notice board.

The final evening must top the entire trip. Precede dinner with an open-bar cocktail party; then have an excellent dinner, and in addition, give every guest a gift to remind each one of this holiday.

When you realize how much money you have made handling your incentive group, you will be eager to repeat the event. Where can you look for more of this type of business?

It's not as hard as you would expect. An enormous amount of money is spent on incentive travel trips, but because the trips actually pay for themselves, everyone is a winner. The participant pays nothing and has a wonderful time; the agent earns magnificently; the corporation, which foots the bill, increases its volume of sales because of the incentive program. It uses only a percentage of the additional income to offset the cost of the trip, so it too has profited.

Suggest this money-making opportunity to your own commerical accounts and to other businesses near you.

A note of caution: before you touch this market at all be sure you know how to handle ordinary group business. An incentive program is group business carried to a much higher level of performance. Get experience with your agency's groups first; then consider this extremely lucrative field.

If you dedicate yourself to this type of business, you would be wise to form an incentive travel unit separate from your regular agency. There is a very practical advantage in doing this. Your incentive travel company can go after business from corporations which already have in-plant offices and commerical accounts with other agencies. They might not want to upset their present agency by dealing with another travel agent, but an incentive travel specialist is a different matter.

By the way, you can use an incentive plan within your own office. Set a target for your own staff to reach, say an increase in your total volume of escorted tours, with a prize of a trip for each employee if the goal is attained.

4—BUSINESS GROUPS

In previous chapters we discussed group travel to vacation destinations as well as commerical accounts. Let us now discuss group travel for businesspeople. They probably won't want to get together on vacation, but there are group business meetings to consider as well as conventions. Many agents will tell you that they handle both, when in actual fact they handle neither. They write airline tickets for the businesspeople attending these events and probably book their hotel space. But they are exceptional if they handle either the full business meeting or the entire convention.

What happens when your corporate accounts calls for a meeting of its key employees from all over the United States (or even from all over the world, if the company is that large)? Most likely each branch office, or its local travel agent, makes the arrangements for its own employees' flights and hotels.

Suppose you suggest to the corporation that it gives you a list of employees who are to attend the meeting. You could then coordinate the entire event—arrange all the flights; situate the businesspeople in a nearby hotel; and arrange for conference rooms, meals, and any other services required. The result would be more convenience for the executives, more control for the corporation, and much more business for you. Let all your corporate accounts know they can benefit by entrusting you with arrangements for their business meetings.

They should discuss with you how "business-oriented" each business meeting is intended to be. Some are pure work sessions; others are a combination of work and relaxation. Choose the destination accordingly. Most large business meetings are planned about three months in advance and last from three to four days.

Conventions are a much larger and more difficult undertaking, and they are outside the range of all but the largest travel agencies. Don't even attempt this type of business if you are not extremely experienced in handling business groups and also have a very sophisticated computer system.

Planning time for conventions ranges upward from three years. The first job is to try to assess approximately (it's not easy), from the various associations sending delegates, how many people are expected to attend. The delegates will come from all over. Perhaps enough of them will come from the same area for you to try to arrange a special air fare. You must be familiar with the basic subject of the convention to be able to answer queries from any participants. Until you are positive that you can handle this type of business, confine yourself to making flight and hotel reservations for executives when they attend conventions.

We have already discussed inbound travel from overseas. Business group travel applies here too. Contact the large business corporations overseas—Volkswagen, Royal Dutch Shell, Imperial Chemical Industries—if you wish to branch out into worldwide business groups. Describe to them in a letter the business groups you have handled in the United States and offer your services for their travel arrangements in this country.

You have already learned that foreign groups require more work because of the language difficulty. The businesspeople coming to the United States from overseas are more likely to speak English than the members of a touring group, but if interpreters are required you should plan to supply them.

The field requires research and detailed work. You

have to anticipate clients' needs and problems and provide what is required. The financial rewards can be great. Corporations pay well to have their meetings run smoothly.

5—THE LUXURY MARKET

The four kinds of travel business we have just looked at can be very rewarding indeed, so rewarding that before you seriously go after these markets you must realize that your agency will have to grow to handle them. This means more employees, more office space, more organization. For most people this expansion of course, is desirable—but not for everyone.

Perhaps specialization appeals to you, and you have the ambition and willingness to work required to make your business stand out from the average agency, but you do not want a large, highly automated operation. You might have just retired from too much responsibility and have no wish to take on as much again; you would like to keep your agency small enough so that it can be handled by just a few people. Also, some clients prefer to deal with a small agency, enjoying the personal service available there.

Seventeen years of travel agency experience leads me to believe that the deluxe market is best served by the small agency. If your agency is in an upper-middle-class area, probably a deluxe business exists there that has not been fully realized. This is a lucrative market that has proved to be resistent to economic downturns.

Travel agents frequently point out that travel is the only industry that constantly sells *down* instead of *up*. In any store the salesperson encourages you to buy the highest-priced item. But in travel we are constantly looking for the lowest possible fare. In fact we are *required* to offer the lowest fare applicable. In the deluxe market, however, the agent has an opportunity to sell upward—higher quality and higher price. This is pleasant selling. The clients know what they're buying, and they're getting their money's worth in service and comfort—well worthwhile in this age of crowded air travel and general mass marketing.

If leisure travel is your strength and you decide to go after the luxury travel market, you must make your office itself a status symbol in your locality. Begin with decoration. If you can afford a decorator, hire one. A well-designed, attractive office is a joy to both client and worker. You could choose one particular color as your trademark, say pale blue; then use that color for all your stationery, clients' itineraries (I do not mean the office work sheets), and luggage tags. This color, along with your logo, should be totally identified with your agency. It should be known throughout the whole area and coveted as a mark of luxury.

Select top-line tour operators for this market, such as Lindblad, Maupintour, Four Winds. You can also approach your luxury clientele with many special offerings: for example, a trip to England in June for the Ascot races, Henley Regatta, and Wimbledon Tennis Championships (don't offer this trip unless you have pre-booked seats—especially for Wimbledon—almost a year ahead).

The safari to Africa is another favorite of the luxury market. If you have a group seriously interested in animals, you could send them to Kenya, Serengeti, Masi Mara Game Lodge, and Treetops. If the group would like more cities and various sightseeing with some good animal viewing as well, send them to South Africa to see beautiful Cape Town, Johannesburg and the gold mines and to Kruger National Park for a day's safari.

The top-quality hotel is another good offering to your deluxe clients. Not only is it beneficial to you in increased commissions, but also you are less likely to have complaints than when you handle lower-priced accommodations. Get to know the choice spots such as Reid's Hotel in Madeira, Sandy Lane Hotel in Barbados, Las Hadas near Manzanillo, Mexico. The luxury client often develops a fondness for a particular hotel and returns frequently.

The cruise lines have not overlooked this area of the travel market. More ships are being built for the smaller, luxury market. Go aboard these ships and actually see the staterooms. You must be sure the cabin you offer is exactly right for your client. Suggest Mediterranean cruises, which tend to be more formal than those to the Caribbean, but choose the shipping line carefully to be sure the clientele is one your client will fit in with comfortably. The Royal Viking Line's around Africa and India cruises are excellent for the sophisticated traveler. They are lengthy, but you can talk to the shipping line and arrange to have your passenger aboard for just a particular section of the cruise.

List on a calendar the dates of your clients' return. Call them the following day and ask about the trip. Such interest pays off. Those clients might soon be calling you back to talk about the next trip.

Affluent clients like to take advantage of the weekend and treat themselves to a change of scene. Suggest a weekend at a luxury hotel. Clients in the suburbs of New York City would love the luxury of a weekend at the Plaza Hotel in New York, with the ease of going to the theater without the trouble of driving home.

This is true in any major city. On the other hand, city residents could reverse the situation and spend a weekend at a delightful country inn. You can make an arrangement with the hotel to include breakfast and dinner and make a single price for the weekend package—all commissionable, of course. These weekends are a lovely break for the client, and again, you have found business that is sure to be repeated.

Selling the luxury market is a very pleasant job. Offer the best and match it with your own excellent service.

18

The World Is Your Office

More than ever we see that the world is indeed shrinking; the problems of one country are becoming the problems of all. When unemployment and the high cost of living are the problems in the United States, so are they in many parts of Europe, the Far East, and other regions around the world. Similarly, when prosperity is enjoyed in the United States we share that happy condition with many of the countries of the Western world.

Before World War II, traveling was largely the prerogative of the wealthy. The British enjoyed the role of the world's most adventurous travelers as they moved between England and the faraway spots of the empire in those days of leisurely travel by ship. Many upper-class English families would return to the same hotel in Switzerland for a month's stay each summer. Elderly English couples of means would spend the winter in the south of France. Perhaps hotel proprietors look back wistfully to those tranquil days when there was time to know their guests and to look forward each year to their return. Today's guest is a stranger, staying an average of two nights at a hotel before rushing on to the next country.

Today most tourists (is it significant, I wonder, that today they are now "tourists" instead of "travelers"?) are not wealthy. Low-cost excursion fares and packages have brought travel within the reach of lower-income groups. In the 1960s the American became the world's number one traveler. As a result, hotels were built to fulfill American requirements for good plumbing, hot water, private bathrooms, heat, and air conditioning.

Prosperity brings movement. No more do international travelers return each year to the same destination and the same hotel. They want to see as much of the world as they can. Americans, after a few visits to Europe and the Caribbean, begin to feel ready for a new experience—the Middle East, perhaps even an African safari. It is almost unbelievable that just over fifty years ago no one had ever flown across the Atlantic Ocean. On May 20 and 21, 1927, Charles Lindberg made the first transatlantic flight from New York to Paris—3,614 miles in 33 hours, 30 minutes, and 29.4 seconds. What a far cry it is from his Spirit of Saint Louis, with no radio communication, to the huge 747s with movies and cocktails and dinner service for 330 people taken for granted.

We have now come full cycle to the statistics quoted in the beginning of this book. The travel industry is one of the fastest growing in the world. It continues to grow despite international economic and financial problems. Today's public has discovered the excitement and satisfaction of seeing other countries, and travel claims a high priority in their spending. The glossy magazines show the jet set at a newly discovered paradise for the rich. And right on their heels, the mass of ordinary tourists will be there. The "good life" is there for all to enjoy.

Early retirement is another recent trend that gives people time to explore the world. Fifty years ago few people considered leaving their native region. Today many people intend to retire abroad in the hope that they will find a peaceful and less expensive way of life.

Throughout the entire world people are now developing a more international outlook. Large business firms are operating not only in the country of their origin but also internationally. The multinational, worldwide firms are growing daily—IBM, Standard Oil, Coca-Cola, Mitsubishi, Nestlé, Volkswagen, Unilever, to mention only a few giants. These large firms send many employees from their home countries all over the world. They also employ thousands of nationals in their host countries. In each instance the employee develops international thinking.

The travel agent is the link between the travel industry and the public.

The agent is at the center of all this movement—flights, information on foreign countries, advice on customs and political attitudes, suitable hotel accommodations. The entire world is literally the travel agents' subject. They must be able to select the right hotel in Sydney, Australia, with the same ease as florists who survey the flowers in their shop and suggest that pink carnations would suit the occasion.

There is no end to the knowledge an agent must constantly acquire. New hotels are being built; whole new resort areas, developed. As people continue to travel one must look harder and harder to find a still secluded beach or a still elite small hotel with superb service.

Travel agents must keep pace with the ever-changing shipping world. From plying the Atlantic, the large passenger liners have switched to cruising the Caribbean. The day of the huge passenger liner as transportation from one continent to another is over. The jet plane has taken over that market now. Today's liners are designed for the cruise market, offering exciting vacations for the average public as well as the very rich, and this market is about to expand dramatically.

Travel agents must be constantly alert and able to absorb the new trends and regulations. There is constant action, an endless flow of people through their offices, and the world is, literally, available for them to see at any time.

In a shrinking world and a rapidly growing industry, the agent's place becomes ever larger and larger. What is a more exciting way to earn a living than in the constant activity of a travel agency; and, then when the pace eases a little, to have a look at your larger office—the world?

Useful Addresses

Federal Aviation Administration
800 Independence Avenue
Washington, D.C. 20591

Civil Aeronautics Board
1825 Connecticut Avenue
Washington, D.C. 20009

Air Traffic Conference of America
1709 New York Avenue, N.W.
Washington, D.C. 20006

Air Transportation Association of America
1709 New York Avenue, N.W.
Washington, D.C. 20006

International Air Transport Association
of America
1000 Sherbrooke Street West
Montreal, P.Q. H3A 2R4

International Passenger Ship Association
17 Battery Place
New York, New York 10004

Pacific Cruise Conference
Pier 35, Suite 200
San Francisco, California 94133

National Railroad Passenger Association (Amtrak)
1 Penn Plaza
New York, New York 10001

Commuter Airline Association of America
1101 Connecticut Avenue
Washington, D.C 20036

American Society of Travel Agents
1300 Nineteenth Street, Suite 230
Washington, D.C. 20036

Association of Retail Travel Agents
8 Maple Avenue
Croton-On-Hudson, New York 10520

Association of Retail Travel Agents,
Western Region
309 Santa Monica Boulevard
Santa Monica, California 90401

Greater Independent Association of National
Travel Services (Giants)
630 Third Avenue
New York, New York 10017

TravelSavers
535 Fifth Avenue
New York, New York 10017

Institute of Certified Travel Agents
148 Linden Street
P.O. Box 56
Wellesley, Massachusetts 02181

Discover America Travel Organization
1899 L Street, N.W.
Washington, D.C. 20036

American Sightseeing International
420 Lexington Avenue
New York, New York 10019

Greyline Sightseeing Association
7 West Fifty-First Street
New York, New York 10001

International Reception Operators
8845 North Olympic Boulevard
Beverly Hills, California 90211

Federation of International Youth
Travel Organizations
81 Island Brygge
2300 Copenhagen Street, Denmark

United States Travel Service
Department of Commerce
Fourteenth and Constitution Avenue, N.W.
Washington, D.C. 20230

Elkort's International Tour Operators' Guide
8845 West Olympic Boulevard
Beverly Hills, California 90211

For International Currency:

Deak Perera:
41 East Forty-Second Street
New York, New York 10017

1800 K Street, Washington, D.C. 20006

17 North Dearborn Street, Chicago, Illinois 60602

Deak & Company:
182 Geary Street
San Francisco, California 94108

Hilton Hotel Center
677 South Figueroa
Los Angeles, California 90017

For worldwide electrical needs:

Franzus Company
352 Park Avenue
New York, New York 10010

All airlines, domestic and international, are listed and
addresses given in the *Official Airline Guides.*

Index